Gardening Basics

Tim Morehouse
Illustrations by Frank Clark

STACKPOLE
BOOKS

Copyright © 1996 by Stackpole Books

Published by
STACKPOLE BOOKS
5067 Ritter Road
Mechanicsburg, PA 17055

Printed in the United States of America

Cover design by Tracy A. Patterson

First edition

10 9 8 7 6 5 4 3 2 1

Library of Congress Cataloging-in-Publication Data

Morehouse, Tim.
    Gardening basics / Tim Morehouse ; illustrations by Frank Clark. — 1st ed.
      p.   cm.
    Includes index.
    ISBN 0-8117-2508-1
    1. Gardening. I. Title.
SB453.M675 1996   95-45232
635.9—dc20   CIP

For my granddaughters,
Sarah Elizabeth and Rachel Grace, who can
"hear the bee about his amorous trade,
Brown in the gypsy-crimson of the rose."
(V. Sackville-West, "The Land")
TIM

For Nancy, my loving partner
May her tuneful garden flourish.
FRANK

Contents

✌

Introduction

ℬ

THE NURSERY OPERATOR'S SLOGAN "A house is not a home until it is planted" is today a part of our way of life. Many of us think of a garden as needing colorful shrubs, ornamental trees, hedges, vines, roses, window boxes, patio containers, and comfortable chairs in which to relax. Of course, all these items must be well fitted to the site and easily cared for.

In this book, you will find information needed by the beginning gardener. To maintain your garden throughout the seasons, you need to know how to weed and water, spray and fertilize, prune and mulch, transplant and stake. At times, although the spirit is willing, the back may be weak. With both the spirit and the back in mind, this book emphasizes a how-to approach. Drawings illustrate step-by-step procedures necessary for accomplishing a given task and encourage gardeners to recognize the potentials of their gardening space.

Where can you acquire the best plants—through mail-order sources or at your local garden center? Is it better to grow your own plants from seed? When and how should you stake perennials? How should you train vines? How do you make compost? How do you install sod? Is laying sod preferable to seeding a lawn? This book answers these questions and more. For the more experienced gardener, the tips included in each chapter may reveal new methods for supporting hard-to-support perennials or cheaper and safer ways to control insects without harming the environment.

In these times of high stress, increased tension, high taxes, and inflation, a place to relax is more important than ever. What can be more pleasing than a garden you design and plant, filled with green things you select and grow from seed or from cuttings? To look at your own handiwork is sufficient reward for the efforts required in maintaining a garden. Enjoy the exercise. You may take many grudges into your garden, but you will never carry one out.

Understanding
Site and Soil

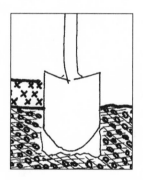

1

Assessing Your Garden Site

ɣ℈

EVERY PLANT has a maximum and minimum temperature range and requires varying amounts of rainfall and sunlight in order to grow; therefore, before you begin gardening activities, you need to determine how much sunlight your property receives during the growing season, its drainage, and whether boggy or marshy areas exist on your site. Learn about the local climate—the average rainfall, the length of the growing season, and the highest and lowest recorded temperatures for your region.

Other gardeners are good sources of information. Before beginning to plan, walk through your neighborhood and look around. If you see a beautiful garden, introduce yourself to the owner and ask questions. What plants grow best in sun and shade in your region? Ask about the local weather patterns and soil. Gardeners are usually more than willing to share their expertise, successes, and failures (along with their extra plants).

Do nothing in haste. A drastic alteration may take years to correct. Wait at least one growing season before making major changes.

Preparing a Site Plan

1. Draw an outline sketch of the site and note the measurements. Also note the dimensions of existing features, such as the house, steps, driveway, garage, storage shed, walks, fences, and trees, and their distances from the boundaries.

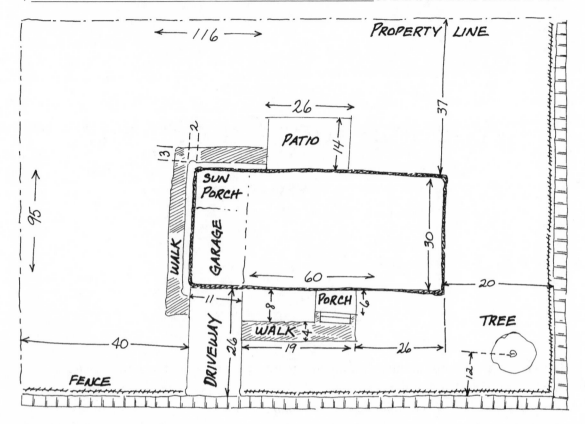

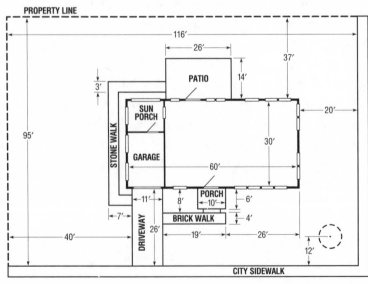

2. Buy graph paper that has ten blocks per inch. Let one small block on the graph paper represent 1 foot. Then 1 inch on your scale drawing will equal 10 feet on the lot. On the graph paper, draw in the boundaries and the exact positions of the house and all existing features you intend to keep.

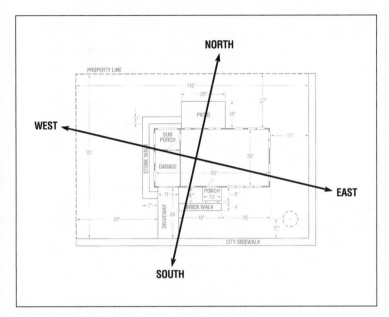

3. Use a compass to locate north on your lot. Cover your scale drawing with a sheet of tracing paper, and draw a north-south line across the center of your house, then an east-west line.

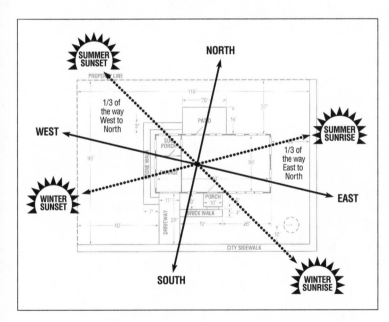

4. Next, draw another line from the center of your house to the margin of the diagram about 1/3 of the way from east to north. Extend this line in the opposite direction for the winter sunset. Draw another line from the center of the diagram to the margin 1/3 of the way from west to north. This line indicates the summer sunset. Extend the line in the opposite direction for the winter sunrise. (This will work for any gardening zone.)

5. Now you need to determine the patterns of sunlight and shade. Walk around your property one weekend during spring or summer and make a record of where the sunlight falls throughout the day. The position of the sun changes throughout the year; it is higher in the sky in summer than in winter—almost straight up at noon in the summer. By looking at a sun diagram of your lot, you can imagine the sun's position throughout the seasons.

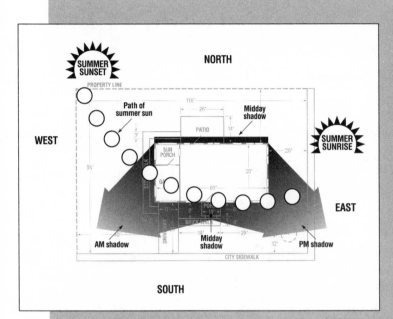

Note that morning shadows fall on the side of a structure opposite the summer sunrise, and evening shadows fall on the side of a structure opposite the summer sunset. Midday a narrow band of shade falls on the north side of a structure.

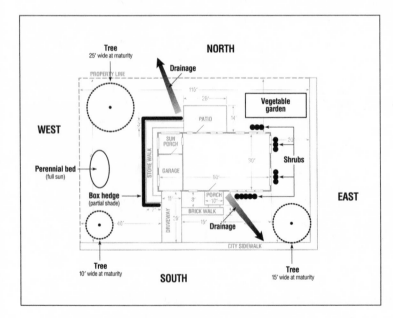

6. Now map out the areas you want to landscape. To note the position of a proposed tree and its spreading branches, draw a circle with a dot in the middle. Use a catalog to determine the mature size of a proposed tree or shrub, and draw your circles to scale. Consider shadows that might fall ten years hence from a mature tree. Also, plot the drainage patterns on your lot, using arrows to indicate water flow.

2

Testing Your Soil

ℰᴢ

SOIL SUSTAINS PLANTS, supplying them with a steady diet of water, air, and important nutrients. Before you plant anything in your garden, you need to test your soil to determine its physical structure (clay, sand, and organic makeup) and its pH—its acidity or alkalinity. The soil's fertility is determined by the amounts of nitrogen (N), phosphorus (P), and potassium (K) present; testing will also tell you how much of these important elements (except nitrogen, which is difficult to measure) your soil contains. In addition, some test results include information about the humus content.

If your soil is not perfect, the next chapter will tell you how to improve what you have.

Soil Types

Most soils contain four different components—clay, silt (fine mineral particles), organic matter, and sand—in varying proportions.

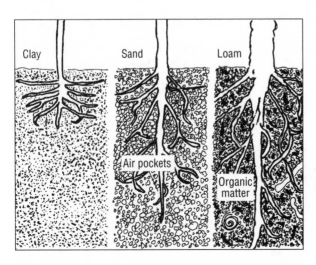

When the soil is damp, judge its texture by scooping out, from a 6-inch depth, a trowelful of topsoil in the area where you intend to garden. Squeeze the soil. Allow several clumps to trickle through your fingers.

If you can form a sticky, gummy ball, your soil is mostly clay. Clay soil contains tiny, fine particles that stick together when wet and act like concrete when dry. If your soil is gritty and thin and trickles through your fingers, it's mostly sand. Sandy soil is light, gritty, porous, and lacking in organic matter. Water quickly fills air spaces but evaporates rapidly. If the soil won't form a ball but is friable (crumbly), dark, and like a piece of chocolate cake, it is loam. Loam is a blend of clay, silt, sand, and organic matter. It is the ideal—what you want to create and maintain on your property.

Soil pH

The pH value of your soil refers to its acidity or alkalinity. Soil pH affects plants mainly by decreasing or increasing their ability to absorb nutrients from minerals present in the soil. The scale for measuring pH runs from 1 to 14. A low reading is acid; a high, alkaline. Somewhere around 7 is the best for most, although not all, gardening. In areas of the country with heavy rainfall of 50 inches or more annually, soils are generally acidic to neutral. In regions where soils have been formed from limestone rocks, they are alkaline. In general, the less rainfall, the more alkaline the soil.

To test your soil pH, buy a soil test kit from a garden center and follow the manufacturer's directions, or send a soil sample to a cooperative extension service. Call or write for instructions on preparing and sending the sample. It is not necessary to buy a pH meter, although these are available at garden centers.

Soil Fertility

Fertility is determined by the ratio of nitrogen, phosphorus, and potassium (N-P-K) present in your soil. These elements are essential for root and leaf growth and flower development. A good soil test kit or a lab test by a cooperative extension service will indicate how fertile your soil is.

Taking a Soil Sample:

To take a soil sample, use a trowel to scrape away any mulch, manure, or litter, and dig 6 inches deep. Scoop one trowelful from at least six different spots where you intend to garden, and dump these into a common bucket. Mix the contents thoroughly. From this mixture, scatter 1 cup of soil onto a cookie sheet to dry in the sun for a day. Then submit your sample to a cooperative extension service or conduct your own test with a kit.

3

Digging and Amending the Soil

℘

YOUR PLANTS ARE ONLY AS GOOD as the soil in which they grow. A rich, loamy soil is the best foundation for healthy lawns, beautiful flowers, and productive vegetable gardens. But not all sites are blessed with the best soil. It is possible, however, to improve what you have by spading in organic matter and nutrients for better texture, porosity, friability, and fertility. Building up your existing soil is a process of gradual replenishment that involves much hard work.

Once you have tested your soil and determined its type and its deficiencies, the next step is to add amendments to enrich its structure and fertility. You'll need some muscle power and a few tools.

TOOLS AND SUPPLIES

Garden spade	Garden rake
Garden shovel	Wheelbarrow
Spading fork	Rotary tiller (optional)

Soil Amendments

Nitrogen is necessary for leaf and stem growth. Well-rotted manure is a good source of nitrogen and also acts as a soil conditioner and improves the soil texture. (*Note:* If you work with manure, it is wise to get a tetanus booster shot if you have not had one within the past ten years.)

If the texture of your soil is good, or if well-rotted manure is not readily available, a less bulky source of nitrogen is cottonseed meal. Fish emulsion is excellent for an immediate source of nitrogen; this can be mixed with water and applied around the base of plants using a watering can. Fish emulsion attracts night-roving animals, however, especially raccoons.

These creatures will uproot your plants in search of fish and can wreck a garden in one night. So don't use fish emulsion if you have these animals in your area.

Phosphorus is important for root development, disease resistance, and fruit and seed production. Apply bone meal or hoof-and-horn meal—good sources of phosphorus—when preparing a permanent bed for perennials, shrubs, or roses.

Potassium is necessary for plant growth and disease resistance. It leaches out quickly, so you may have to make applications each growing season. Wood ashes from a stove or fireplace work well. Other sources of potassium include chicken grit (the "starter" mix), which is simply crushed granite, and greensand, a mineral deposit from the sea.

To lighten heavy clay soil, add perlite or vermiculite. The porous granules of these substances absorb and help distribute fertilizers and water, and provide aeration. It's also good to add generous quantities of peat moss and compost.

Tilling the Soil

Avoid working in soil that is too wet or too dry. Use a spade to turn one shovelful, and try to break up the clod. If it crumbles easily, it's time to cultivate. If it's too sticky, wait several days.

1. Clear away any debris that should not be incorporated into the bed, such as viable weeds, grass, large sticks, and stones. Divide the bed into rows, and dig one row at a time. Use a garden spade if you need to slice through sod. A garden shovel is best for turning compacted soil, and a garden fork is best for sandy or loamy soils. Turn each shovelful or spadeful on its side.

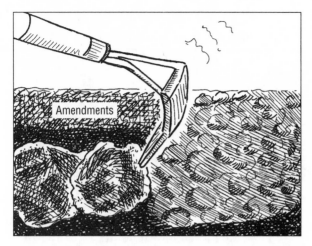

2. Scatter your amendments, such as organic fertilizers, peat moss, or compost, over the freshly cultivated area. Use generous quantities—at least a 4- to 6-inch layer. Use a garden rake to break up the clods and to blend the amendments, then smooth the surface of your garden.

If your soil is too heavy to dig by hand, or the area is too large, use a rotary tiller, and spread your amendments *before* cultivating.

Double-digging

Double-digging is a process that incorporates air and organic matter, along with the amendments, into your soil, where they become readily available to the roots. This technique is especially useful for growing vegetables, but it's not necessary for ornamental planting.

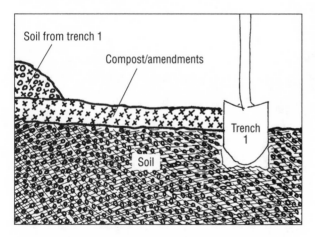

1. Spread compost or other soil amendments 4 to 6 inches deep over the area where you plan to double-dig. With shovel or spade, dig a trench 1 foot wide and the depth of your tool. Remove this soil and pile it at the end of the bed.

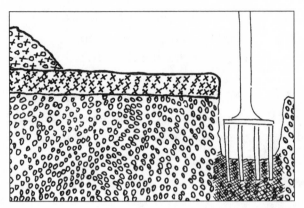

2. Loosen the soil in the bottom of this trench using a spade or garden fork.

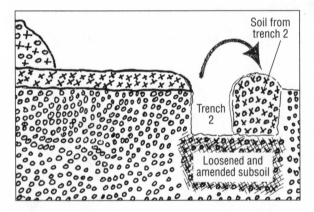

Soil from trench 2

Trench 2

Loosened and amended subsoil

3. Dig a second trench next to the first one, shoveling the soil forward into the first trench. Mix soil and amendments together with your spade as you progress. Break up any clods with a spade or garden fork. Loosen the soil in the bottom of the second trench.

Soil from first trench

Last trench

4. Continue the procedure. When you reach the last trench, fill it with the soil you removed from the first.

If you are moving into a new home built on a subdivision lot, you may find that the contractors have spread yellow subsoil over your property (including a backfill for the foundations). This subsoil comes from basement excavations. Often only a thin layer of topsoil is spread over this subsoil before the lawn is seeded. Plants will not flourish in yellow subsoil. Adding amendments is important. You have two options:

1. Hire a contractor to remove the yellow subsoil to a depth of 14 to 18 inches and replace it with good topsoil. This is an expensive investment (beware of "bargain" soil), but it provides a lifetime of successful gardening.

2. Purchase sphagnum peat moss, manure, vermiculite, perlite, and gypsum. Collect shredded leaves and compost. Add these soil amendments equal to 25 to 50 percent of the total soil volume in the areas where you intend to garden. Mix it in. The soil level will be higher, but the organic matter will break down over time. These amendments will improve aeration and drainage; plant roots can then grow through your soil and obtain the nutrients.

If you are having a home designed and built, ask the contractor about the soil. To save yourself much time and labor, add a contractual stipulation that will guarantee good topsoil around your home's foundation and in areas where you intend to garden.

4

Composting

COMPOSTING IS THE NATURAL BIOLOGICAL PROCESS of decomposition that converts any organic material into a humuslike soil conditioner. All soil types benefit from annual additions of compost. As your lawn debris (grass clippings, leaves, twigs) and kitchen scraps break down, a rich dark crumbly material forms. The process may take a few weeks to several years, depending on the size of the materials you start with and the method you use.

What happens when you compost? The remains of plants contain various amounts of plant food. They are broken down in a rotting process carried out by bacteria, fungi, microbes, microorganisms, and earthworms. As decomposition takes place, heat is generated that assists in the breakdown. As the plant remains rot and become compost, they fix nitrogen from the air through a bacteria species known as *Azotobacter*. This nitrogen is used by plants when you apply the finished compost to the garden. The biological breakdown of garden refuse also produces antibiotics that attack and kill harmful nematodes and other soil organisms that cause damage by feeding on plant roots.

Earthworms are an important part of the decomposition process and the finished product. They aerate your compost, enrich it with their castings, and help break down organic matter into smaller granules. They also produce a wide range of enzymes that benefit the bacteria at work.

Some people prefer to build a passive compost pile over a period of time; others prefer to use containers, in which the compost ingredients rot much faster. The size of your compost pile will depend on the size of your garden. Containers in many types and sizes are available at garden centers. Whether you build your own, buy one, or simply construct a pile out back, make certain it's easily accessible.

Compost Ingredients

The following ingredients can all be added to your compost:

• Pruned, shredded, and chipped branches, twigs, and any organic yard litter. Small pieces break down faster.

• Grass clippings. It's best to add them in layers no more than 3 inches deep or mix them thoroughly with other debris so that they will not turn into slime. If your lawn has been treated with herbicides, however, do not add the clippings to the compost heap.

• Leaves. A fifty-fifty mixture of dried and green, randomly applied, will feed and aerate your compost.

• Straw, weeds, and any other garden refuse. Don't worry about weed seeds; the heat generated in the composting process will kill them.

• Kitchen scraps, including peelings, eggshells, teabags, and coffee grounds, along with paper filters. Don't add meat scraps or bones; they may attract rodents.

• Water. This is an essential compost ingredient, especially if you add straw or any green material.

Binless, or Passive, Composting

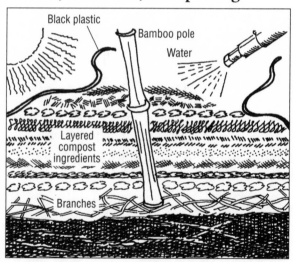

For thousands of years, gardeners worldwide have used the passive method of composting. Begin by placing branches on the ground, crisscrossing them and covering the area where you intend to build your pile. This foundation will let air circulate under your pile, assisting in the decomposition process. Covering your heap with plastic sheeting will hasten decay by trapping heat inside and preventing loss of moisture. Apply water occasionally; simply pull back the plastic cover and hose down.

Another aeration method comes from the ancient Chinese, who built their passive compost heaps around a vertical pipe or sturdy bamboo pole. They simply wiggled the pole from time to time to supply air to the bottom of the pile. If you suffer from back problems, take advantage of this wisdom.

Composting Containers

Wire Containers

Wire compost bins are made from galvanized metal mesh. Some have a PVC coating. Buy a bin that is sturdy; the smaller the gauge of the wire, the sturdier the cage will be. To make your own wire composter, drive four 4-foot poles into the ground in a 3-foot square, and stretch chicken wire (a 12-foot length) around the poles. You can build several such bins side by side if you have the space.

Wooden Bins

Wooden bins come in two varieties. Some are made of long, thin boards stacked horizontally like a log house; others have sides made of solid boards. The drawback to a wooden bin is that the wood may rot and warp. Models made from redwood or cedar are best. Avoid pressure-treated wood, which may leach arsenic into your compost. Wooden bins often come in two or three sections so that you can use one for finished compost and another for compost in progress. This keeps the cycle moving.

Plastic Bins

Plastic containers usually hold 3 cubic feet of compost and have a solid, fitted lid that lifts open easily but keeps rain out. There is usually a sliding panel at the bottom that you can open in order to scoop out finished compost. The sides have holes for ventilation. Some of these bins are made from recycled plastic, and even the screws holding the bin together are plastic and won't rust. The gray, black, brown, or green plastic absorbs the sun's rays and heats up quickly to promote bacterial digestion inside the bin.

Rotating Bins

Rotating bins are plastic or wooden drums that spin and rotate top-to-bottom from the midpoint of their long axis. There are holes in the sides for aeration. Sliding panels enable you to empty and fill the bins with ease. Either end should tip easily into a wheelbarrow. They heat up quickly and are easily turned and aerated, and they make compost in a short time—the manufacturers say within twenty-one days.

Many city waste departments are now charging for hauling away leaves and garden refuse, and some cities will not pick it up at curbside. Why not compost your garden waste? Your garden will be more productive and disease-free because you amend your beds with compost. You will be protecting your plants without costly and dangerous chemicals, and the earth—as well as your backyard—will be richer, more productive, and more beautiful for your efforts.

Composting Tips

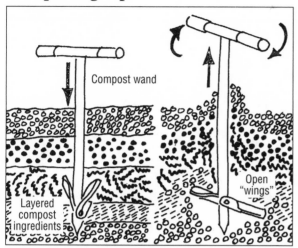

Compost wand

Open "wings"

Layered compost ingredients

• Aerate a passive pile every two or three weeks and a bin type once a month during the summer and fall, using a pitchfork, spade, or compost wand. A compost wand is a slender pole with collapsing butterfly wings at the tip. To use it, push the wand downward in the center of the pile as far as it will go, then pull upward. The wings open, and the compost is mixed as you extract the wand.

• Water the pile occasionally. A thorough soaking every few days in hot, dry weather will provide the moisture needed for the bacterial breakdown of materials. A garden hose should be within easy reach of your composting area.

• Keep buckets of rotted farmyard manure, rotted sawdust, and topsoil nearby, and add a shovelful occasionally to enrich your compost and hasten the decomposition process.

• Add a few handfuls of a dry, all-purpose fertilizer (5-10-5 or 10-10-10) and lime to your passive heap once a month. This will assist in the decomposition process. You can do the same with a tumbler or bin to augment the supply of nitrogen.

• Alternate additions of green and dried debris. If this is not always possible in the home garden, just put in what you have when you have it.

• If your pile smells, it's oxygen starved. Alternate dried and green refuse, and aerate more frequently.

Don't worry—even if you don't follow all the above suggestions, you will eventually have usable, valuable compost filled with squirming, red compost worms.

When your compost is done, it should be brown and crumbly with a sweet woodsy smell. Different materials break down at different rates, however, so some semifibrous material may still be present. Use this material along with the finished compost, or leave it a bit longer to decompose.

In southern states, compost can be made in three months; in northern states, about six months. Again, this depends on the size of your additions and the weather. Begin composting when you start to mow the lawn in early spring, and try to make use of your finished compost by late fall.

Starting Seeds and Propagating Plants

Sowing Seeds Indoors

IT IS FUN AND ECONOMICAL to start seeds of flowering plants and some vegetables indoors. You can grow annual bedding plants, biennials, and perennials, as well as unusual Chinese vegetables for stir-fry. You will be saving money and will avoid the crowds at the garden centers. Planting your own seeds gives you control over their growing conditions—no wind, cold, or drought. You can control the amount of light and heat they receive and keep them free of competition from larger, established plants. What's more, your seeds are sheltered from diseases and insects. In other words, you provide the best conditions for seeds to germinate, and success is almost virtually guaranteed.

When the seed catalogs arrive in December and January, indulge yourself. Order your vegetable and flower seeds early, and plant indoors. You can enjoy the pleasures of gardening on a windowsill or under lights long before winter has gone. Once spring arrives and all danger of frost has vanished, transplant your seedlings in the garden.

TOOLS AND SUPPLIES

Store-bought trays, or flats, and containers at least 2 inches deep with holes in the bottom

Liquid household bleach

Bucket

Perlite, vermiculite, and Canadian sphagnum peat moss, or a commercial seed-starting mix

Spray bottle

Paper towels

Plastic wrap

Seed flats, or trays for starting seeds, are available at garden centers. For containers, you can use cottage cheese cartons, yogurt cups, or Styrofoam coffee cups. Such things as the bottoms of plastic milk cartons (with the top three-quarters cut off) are suitable if you punch drainage holes in the bottom and scrub them thoroughly in a weak solution of liquid bleach in hot water.

Sowing Seeds

Always read the directions for sowing and the cultural information on the backs of seed packets. Refrigerate (but do not freeze) packets of flower seeds one week before sowing to hasten germination. You can purchase a commercial seed-starting mix or make your own from equal parts vermiculite, perlite, and sphagnum peat moss.

1. Dump your starting mix in a pile in the center of a work table or fill a bucket two-thirds full. Set aside a container full of dry soil mixture for covering your seeds after planting. Make a well in the center of the soil and fill it with water. Mix thoroughly until all particles are wet.

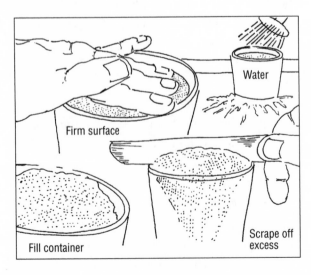

Water

Firm surface

Fill container

Scrape off excess

2. Fill your containers with the moistened soil. Scrape off excess soil with a kitchen knife or ruler, then lightly firm the mixture into place with your fingers. Water, and allow your containers to drain for a few minutes.

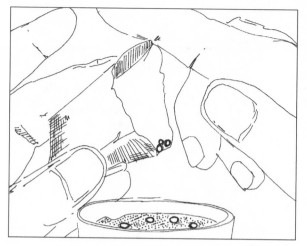

3. Crimp your seed packet into a **V**, and then tap out the seeds using your index finger. Try to space the seeds evenly over the surface of your soil mix. If you are sowing very fine seeds, such as petunias, mix the seeds with fine silver sand so that they will spread more evenly. To make silver sand, sift builder's sand through a sieve and use the finest granules. Place a teaspoon of these fine granules into the seed packet, gently shake, then empty the mixture by tapping out the contents.

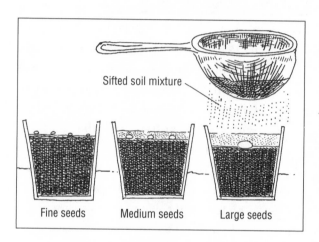

Sifted soil mixture

Fine seeds   Medium seeds   Large seeds

4. Fine seeds, the size of ground pepper, should not be covered. Seeds a little larger, the size of rice, should barely be covered. Large seeds need to be covered just so that they cannot be seen. Cover the seeds by sifting some of the dry mixture through a strainer and shaking it over the surface of the containers.

Paper towel

5. Water the containers by placing a piece of paper towel over the container or seed flat and then sprinkling water on top of it. After the water soaks through and runs out of the drainage holes of your containers, remove the paper towel and stretch sheets of plastic wrap over each container.

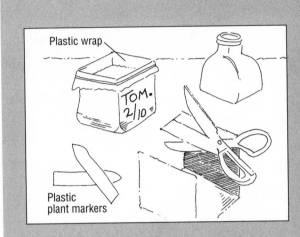

Use a waterproof marker or pencil to label each container with the name of the plant and the date sown. Be meticulous about this to avoid confusion later. Make your own plant tags by cutting strips 6 inches long by 3/4 inch wide from white plastic bleach bottles or plastic milk cartons.

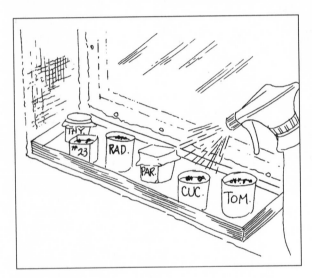

6. Place your containers in a window but out of direct sunlight. After the seeds germinate, discard the plastic wrap. Check your seedlings daily. Mist lightly with a spray bottle when the soil mixture feels dry. Do not allow the soil to dry out or to become soggy. After leaves begin to appear, place the seedlings in direct sunlight. If there is a chance that sunlight might scorch and damage delicate leaves, provide some shade during the hottest time of day. Use newspaper or a translucent sheet.

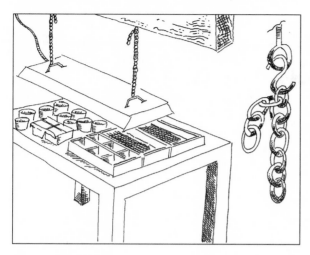

7. To provide additional light, you may use a two- or three-tube 40-watt industrial fluorescent fixture with a reflector and pink or cool white bulbs. Suspend your fixture 6 to 8 inches above the containers. As the seedlings grow, raise the fixture. Use a timer to provide 12 to 14 hours of light daily, or leave the lights on around the clock. Plants are not affected adversely by full-time lighting.

Transplanting

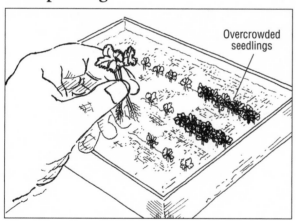

Overcrowded seedlings

1. When your seedlings are about 1 inch tall (you do not have to wait until true leaves appear), pick out overcrowded seedlings. Gently lift each seedling or tiny clump of seedlings with your fingers or a kitchen fork.

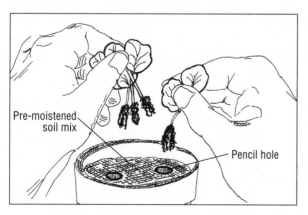

Pre-moistened soil mix

Pencil hole

2. Break apart the thinned clump, and transplant individual seedlings 1 or 2 inches apart in containers filled with fresh, premoistened soil mix. Poke a pencil into the soil mix to make a tiny hole, gently insert the seedling, and push soil mix around the roots.

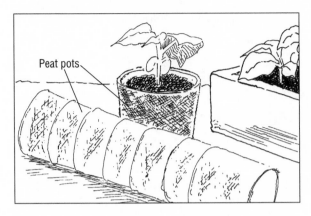

Peat pots

3. Use peat pots for vining plants, such as cucumber, squash, and tomato seedlings, so that they can be placed directly into the garden without disturbing the root systems.

DATE OUT IN

4. Before transplanting indoor seedlings in the garden, harden them off by exposing them to the outdoors in a limited way. Place them in a sheltered area out of direct sunlight and wind, such as on a porch, patio, or deck, for two or three hours each day when the temperatures are well above freezing. Do this for three or four days. If you are not home during the day, place them outside for a few hours in the late afternoon when you come home from work, but bring them inside overnight.

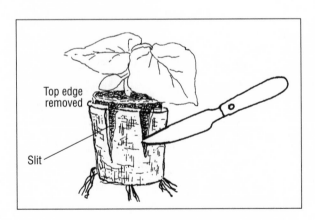

Top edge removed

Slit

5. After hardening off, seedlings are ready for transplanting outdoors. Tear off the top inch of the peat pots before transplanting in the garden. Do this to prevent the pot from acting like a wick. Using a knife, make two or three slits in the sides of the peat containers to allow moisture to reach the roots more quickly.

6

Sowing Seeds Outdoors

❧

THE CHEAPEST METHOD for raising plants is to sow seeds directly into the prepared soil of your garden. Many annuals, herbaceous perennials, biennials, and vegetables can be successfully grown this way. If you want to raise your vegetables organically, you really must sow your own seed, since finding vegetable seedlings raised without chemical sprays and fertilizers is next to impossible.

There is no magic involved in sowing seeds. If you are aware of a plant's sensitivity to frost—especially necessary for spring planting—and exercise common sense regarding soil temperature for proper germination, you can't go wrong.

Annuals are plants that complete their growth cycle in one year and should be started from seed each year. Here are some easy-to-grow varieties:

China aster *(Callistephus chinensis)*
Gaillardia *(Gaillardia pulchella)*
Marigold (*Tagetes* spp.)
Morning glory *(Ipomoea imperialis)*
Nasturtium *(Tropaeolum majus)*
Portulaca *(Portulaca grandiflora)*
Sweet alyssum *(Lobularia maritima)*
Sweet pea *(Lathyrus odoratus)*
Zinnia (*Zinnia* spp.)

Perennials are plants whose roots live in the ground from year to year even though the foliage may die down in the fall. Easy-to-grow varieties include these plants:

Balloon flower *(Platycodon grandiflorus)*

Bee balm (*Monarda* spp.)

Cardinal flower *(Lobelia cardinalis)*

Columbine (*Aquilegia* spp.)

Coreopsis (*Coreopsis* spp.)

Forget-me-not (*Myosotis* spp.)

Primrose (*Primula* spp.)

Shasta daisy *(Chrysanthemum maximum)*

Hardy candytuft *(Iberis sempervirens)*

Biennials are plants that take two growing seasons to complete their life cycle. They make part of their growth one year, bloom the next year, then set seed and die. Easy-to-grow varieties include the following:

Canterbury Bell *(Campanula medium)*

Foxglove *(Digitalis purpurea)*

Hollyhock *(Althaea rosea)*

Honesty *(Lunaria annula)*

Sweet William *(Dianthus barbatus)*

TOOLS AND SUPPLIES

Shovel or spade   Gypsum or lime (optional)

Garden rake   String and stakes (optional)

Garden hoe   Compost or growing medium

Watering can

Planting Seeds

First prepare the soil as directed in chapter 3. To determine the best time to sow in your region, read the backs of the seed packets. Wait until all danger of frost has passed and the soil has started to warm up. It should be at the crumbly stage. Soak hard-coated seeds, such as morning glory and sweet pea, overnight in a glass of water to hasten germination.

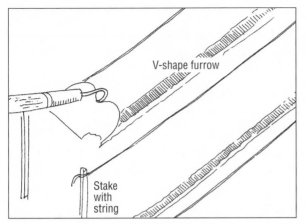

1. If you are planting in straight rows, make a **V**-shaped furrow down the row with a hoe. Stretch a string between stakes for neater results. If you are planting in a random fashion (as in the front of a flower border) or in hills, use your finger to poke holes for the seeds. Seeds planted too deep or too shallow will not germinate, so check the seed packets for correct planting depths. Lightly water the holes or furrows, then drop the seeds in place following the guidelines on the seed packets for proper spacing.

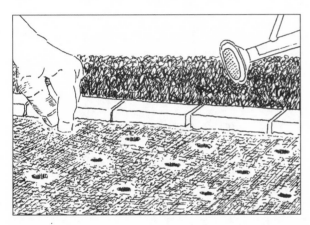

2. Cover the seeds with a growing medium (professional soil mix) or sifted compost. This will offer less resistance than garden soil to the seedlings when they germinate. Press the soil firmly into place with your hands or tamp it down with the back of your garden hoe. Label your plantings.

Thinning Seedlings

When seedlings are several inches high and two pairs of true leaves have developed (the first set of leaves are cotyledons, or seed leaves), thin overcrowded areas.

1. Insert a kitchen fork into the soil where you're thinning, and lift out a clump of excess seedlings. Gently tease the seedlings apart, and discard what you don't need. Be ruthless about this to prevent overcrowding.

2. If your seedlings are so crowded that by removing one you will disturb too many others, snip off the unwanted seedlings with a pair of scissors.

Transplanting Seedlings

Rather than discarding thinned seedlings, you may want to transplant special varieties to increase your supply. In fact, most ornamentals and leaf vegetables can be moved and transplanted easily. Root crops may fork if transplanted, however.

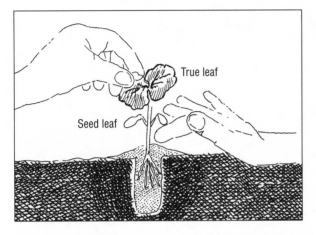

1. Poke holes in prepared soil according to the spacing suggested on the seed packet, inserting your finger deep enough for the roots. Handle the leaves only; stems bruise easily, and this may invite fungus attack. Insert the seedling, then tamp the soil gently around the roots. Water all transplanted seedlings gently but thoroughly.

2. If you are transplanting on a sunny day, protect the transplants from the hot sun by covering them with boxes, newspaper cones, or bushel baskets. After a day or two, remove the covers.

7

Taking Cuttings

ฦ

IF YOU WANT TO INCREASE your supply of a favorite plant—or obtain one you covet from a neighbor's garden—take cuttings. Starting new plants from parts of established ones will save you money, and although seeds do not necessarily come true, rooted cuttings always produce the same characteristics as the parent.

Softwood stem cuttings are those taken from semihard wood or from greenwood produced when the plant is actively growing in the spring or early summer); *hardwood* stem cuttings are those taken when the plant is dormant in the fall. Softwood cuttings root in a matter of weeks; hardwood cuttings are slower and require patience—sometimes a year's worth. Some hardwood plants do not root and should be started from seed. These include fruit trees (which are grafted), nut trees, maples, oaks, birches, and beeches. If in doubt, ask a county extension agent for advice. The techniques for propagating both kinds of stem cuttings are simple, and the success rate is usually 80 percent.

New plants also can be grown from leaf cuttings taken from fleshy-leaved plants, such as Rex begonias, gloxinias, African violets, and tuberous begonias. Root cuttings, taken from Oriental poppies, blackberries, raspberries, and other plants whose roots sprout, are easily propagated to increase your stock.

Taking and Rooting Softwood Cuttings

Herbaceous plants without a persistent woody stem (perennials whose tops die down to the ground in winter), such as dahlias, roses, bigleaf hydrangeas, chrysanthemums, penstemons, lavender, and asters, are easily increased through softwood cuttings.

TOOLS AND SUPPLIES

Flowerpots 4 to 6 inches deep or wooden
   or plastic flats with holes for drainage,
   4 inches deep
Glass jars or clear plastic food bags

Coarse builder's sand, peat moss, vermiculite
Sharp knife, hand pruners, or scissors
Rooting hormone (available at garden
   centers)

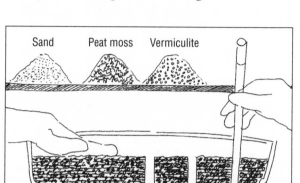

1. Mix equal parts premoistened sand, peat moss, and vermiculite. Fill flowerpots or plastic or wooden flats, and tamp down lightly by hand. The rooting mixture should be $1/2$ inch from the top. Using a pencil, poke holes 2 inches deep and 2 inches apart in the mixture.

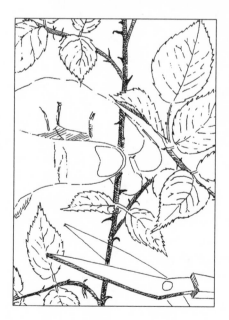

2. Take cuttings early in the day using a sharp knife or scissors. For herbaceous (nonwoody) plants, cut a piece of side branch at least 3 to 5 inches long with two leaf buds. For a softwood cutting of a shrub, use pruners to cut an 8-inch piece of pliable yet mature growth. The cut should be below a leaf bud or joint of a stem, but any place between buds is satisfactory.

3. Strip the leaves off the lower third of the cutting. If the remaining leaves are quite large, cut back part of the leaf surface to lessen transpiration and to provide more room for cuttings in the container. Place them in a jar of water out of sunlight or in a plastic bag in the vegetable crisper of the refrigerator until you are ready to proceed.

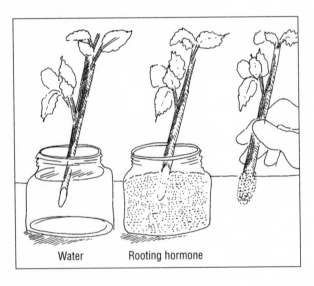

Water   Rooting hormone

4. Dip $1/2$ inch of the cut stem into water, then into hormone powder. Shake off any excess powder.

5. Insert the cuttings into the holes you have poked in the soil mix. Use your fingers to firm the potting mixture around each cutting. Water gently to settle.

6. Cover the cuttings with clean glass jars or plastic bags. Temperatures around the cuttings should be about 70 degrees F. Place the cuttings in a well-lighted area, but not in direct sunlight.

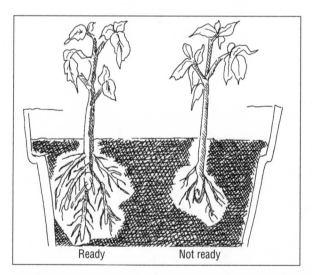

Ready   Not ready

7. Check your cuttings every two weeks. Gently tug on the top of a cutting to see if roots have formed. Lift one out. When roots are $1^1/_2$ inches long, the cutting is ready to transplant. If rooted by midsummer, plant the cuttings directly in the garden; if they don't root until late fall, place the cuttings in a cold frame and plant in permanent locations the following spring.

If you are visiting another garden and are offered cuttings, ask your host for a potato. Poke holes in the potato, then insert the cuttings. The moisture in the spud will preserve them for twenty-four hours and give you time to prepare for doing things properly.

Taking and Rooting Hardwood Cuttings

Take cuttings of such plants as forsythia, weigela, mock orange, lilac, spirea, viburnum, and deutzia in late fall after the plants go dormant. Because root growth is slow, you may have to transplant hardwood cuttings the following spring in coarse sand and wait until roots form.

TOOLS AND SUPPLIES

Hand pruners	Plastic wrap, muslin, or piece of glass
Sharp knife	Coarse builder's sand
Wooden box	Rooting hormone

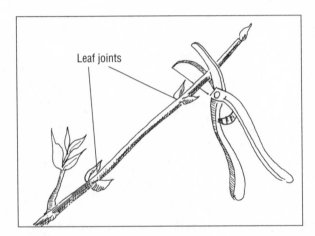

1. Using pruners, cut the tip of a branch back to where the wood is the thickness of a pencil. Make cuttings 6 to 9 inches long, and include two leaf joints.

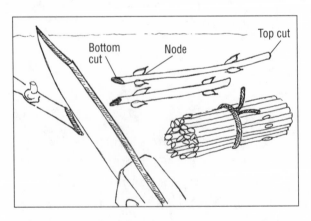

2. Then, using a sharp knife or pruners, make the bottom cuts slanted just below a node. Cut the tops even so that you can distinguish top from base. Tie your cuttings in bundles, and label each bundle with the date and plant variety.

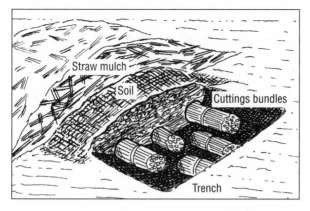

3. Place the bundles in a trench and cover them with 2 inches of soil. Before the ground freezes, mulch the trench with 8 inches of straw or hay. There is no need for supplementary watering during the winter.

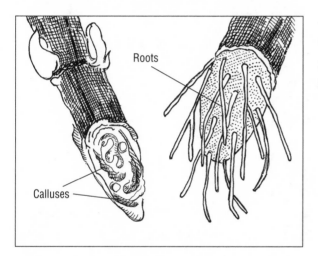

4. In the spring, remove hardwood cuttings from their trench. Some will have formed calluses, and others will have tiny roots.

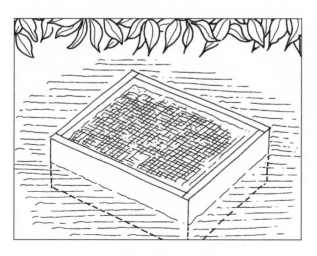

5. Place a wooden box, with the bottom removed, halfway into the ground out of direct sunlight. Fill it with 5 to 6 inches of clean, coarse builder's sand.

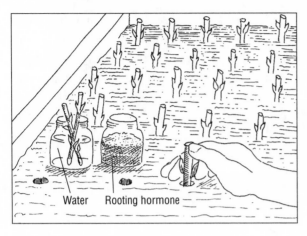

Water   Rooting hormone

6. Dip the slanted ends of the cuttings into water first, then hormone powder. Using a pencil, make holes in the sand 3 inches deep and 2 to 4 inches apart. Insert cuttings into the holes, and firm the sand around them. Water thoroughly but gently.

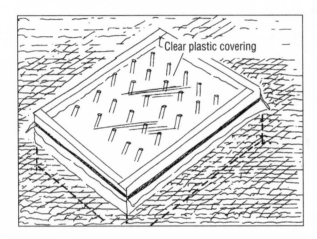

Clear plastic covering

7. Cover the top of the box with plastic wrap, muslin, or a piece of glass.

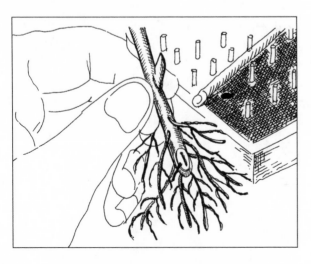

8. Root growth may take several months. Keep the sand moist but not waterlogged. Test for root growth by examining a cutting every 2 to 3 weeks. When roots are 2 inches long, transplant cuttings to permanent locations.

Taking Root Cuttings

Plants are easily propagated from root cuttings of Oriental poppy, plumbago, Japanese anemone, Siberian bugloss, bleeding heart, blackberry, and raspberry.

TOOLS AND SUPPLIES

Large pot or flat
Sandy garden soil or commercial potting mixture
Piece of glass or plastic wrap

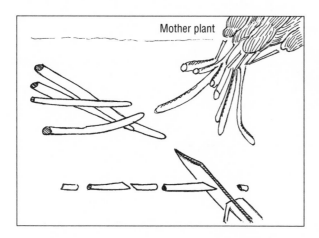

1. Select a healthy plant. Lift it out of the soil, and cut off roots $3/16$ to $3/8$ inch in diameter and 2 inches long. Unless you are willing to sacrifice the mother plant, do not cut more than a half dozen cuttings, depending on the size of the root system. Replant the mother.

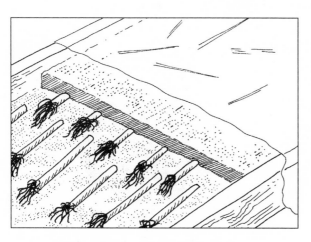

2. Lay cuttings 2 inches apart in a horizontal position on top of a flat or large pot filled with sandy garden soil or a commercial potting mixture. Cover them with $1/2$ inch of additional soil. Firm soil by hand. Moisten thoroughly, and cover with a piece of glass or plastic. Place containers in the shade. Transplant when tiny sprouts have emerged.

Taking and Rooting Leaf Cuttings

Fleshy-stemmed plants such as gloxinias, African violets, Rex begonias, peperomia, jade plants, and sedums root easily from leaf cuttings.

TOOLS AND SUPPLIES

Pot 4 to 5 inches wide   Rooting hormone (optional)

Sharp knife or razor blade   Coarse sand

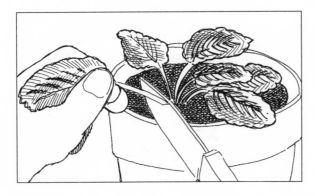

1. Using a sharp knife or razor blade, cut a young leaf with 1 to 2 inches of stem attached. Make a slanted cut at the end of the stem.

2. Dip in water and then rooting hormone if you wish, then insert 1 inch of the stem with leaf attached into premoistened coarse sand. Water thoroughly, and cover with plastic wrap. Place pot in a warm, well-lighted place. Keep soil moist but not waterlogged.

3. When tiny leaves form at the base of the stem, the leaf cutting is ready to be transplanted.

New growth

8

Dividing Perennials

❧

MOST PERENNIALS SHOULD BE DIVIDED every two to four years in order to rejuvenate them. This will cause them to bloom more vigorously. If your clumps show signs of dying at the center, if they produce weak, less-than-perfect blooms, or if they are crowding out other plantings, it is time to divide. Division will also increase your supply.

The best time to divide is when the plant is dormant—either in early spring before rapid growth begins or after the plant has flowered. If you divide in late summer after flowering, do so while your plants still have several months to settle in before winter begins. If your area has early winters, always divide in the spring.

Some perennials are shallow-rooted and require frequent division; others require division every two or three years; still others resent division and do not need frequent dividing. Here are guidelines for some common plants.

Plants That Require Frequent Division
Aster (*Aster novae-angliae* and *A. novi-belgii*)
Bee balm (*Monarda didyma*)
Blanketflower (*Gaillardia aristata* and *G.* x *grandiflora*)
Boltonia (*Boltonia* spp.)
Chrysanthemum (*Chrysanthemum* x *morifolium*)
False dragonhead (*Physostegia virginiana*)
Fleabane (*Erigeron speciosus*)
Golden marguerite (*Anthemis* spp.)
Hardy ageratum (*Eupatorium coelestinum*)
Lily-of-the-valley (*Convallaria majalis*)

Sneezeweed *(Helenium autumnale)*
Snow-in-summer *(Cerastium tomentosum)*
Yarrow *(Achillea ptarmica)*

Plants That Require Division Every Two or Three Years

Avens (*Geum* spp.)
Canterbury bells (*Campanula* spp.)
Coral bells *(Heuchera sanguinea)*
Cornflower (*Centaurea* spp.)
Daylily (*Hemerocallis* spp.)
Iris (*Iris* spp.)
Lungwort (*Pulmonaria* spp.)
Peony (*Paeonia* spp.)
Phlox (*Phlox* spp.)
Primrose *(Primula polyantha)*
Speedwell (*Veronica* spp.)
Spirea *(Astilbe arendsii)*
Sunflower (*Helianthus* spp.)

Plants That Resent Division

These plants do not need frequent division. If they must be divided, do so when they are completely dormant.

Anemone *(Anemone x hybrida)*
Baby's breath *(Gypsophila paniculata)*
Balloon flower *(Platycodon grandiflorus)*
Bleeding heart *(Dicentra spectabilis)*
Bugloss *(Anchusa italica)*
Butterfly weed *(Asclepias tuberosa)*
Christmas rose and Lenten rose (*Helleborus niger* and *H. orientalis*)
False indigo (*Baptisia* spp.)
Gas plant *(Dictamnus albus)*
Lupine (*Lupinus* spp.)
Monkshood (*Aconitum* spp.)
Oriental poppy *(Papaver orientale)*
Red-hot poker *(Kniphofia uvaria)*
Sea holly (*Eryngium* spp.)
Virginia bluebells *(Mertensia virginica)*

Preparing the New Bed

Prepare the new bed where you will plant your divisions before digging up old, overgrown clumps of perennials. This way, you can transplant before the root divisions dry out or are damaged by exposure to sun and wind. Turn over the soil in the new bed to a depth of 10 inches. Incorporate several inches of compost, damp Canadian sphagnum peat moss, well-rotted manure, and—if your soil is heavy, sticky clay—some pea gravel or sharp sand.

TOOLS AND SUPPLIES

Garden spade

Garden fork (some perennial clumps require two forks for dividing)

Sharp knife

Garden shears or kitchen scissors

Liquid household bleach

Dividing Shallow-rooted Plants

Divide shallow-rooted perennials, such as violets, daisies, phlox, and chrysanthemums as follows.

1. Lift the clump with a spade.

2. Using both hands, break off sections from the mother plant for replanting.

Discard dying center

3. If the clump is a mass of heavily matted, intertwined roots, use a sharp knife to sever the crown into sections.

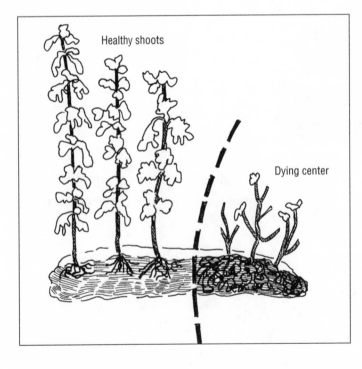

Healthy shoots

Dying center

4. Always make certain that you have two or more healthy growing shoots, plus roots in each section. Discard the dying center of each clump you divide.

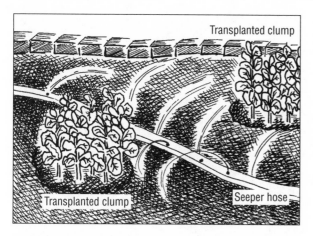

5. Transplant the divisions to the prepared bed and water well, but don't flood the bed.

Dividing Daylilies

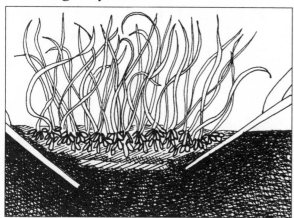

1. Dig around the clump with a garden spade, and lift it out.

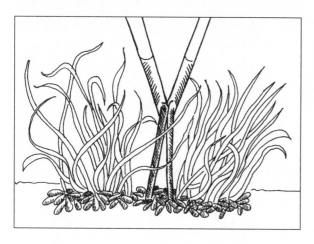

2. If the clump is heavily overgrown, push two garden forks, back-to-back, into the middle of the crown. Pull the forks apart in opposite directions to break the clump into two halves. This may take several attempts.

3. Pull the section apart by hand.

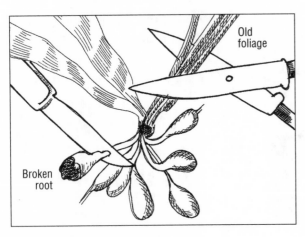

4. Shear off the old foliage of each division. Trim off any broken roots with a sharp knife.

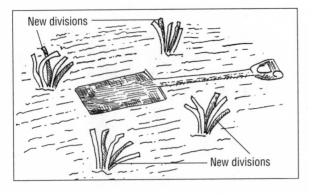

5. For a new, healthy, blooming-size planting, form a circle with three or four fan divisions. Space the groupings 12 to 18 inches apart, and transplant the divisions at the level of the original plant.

6. Water well, but don't flood the bed.

Dividing Bearded Iris Rhizomes

1. Lift the clump with a garden fork and wash the soil from the plants.

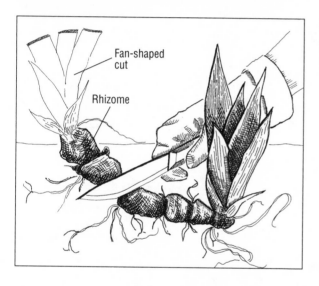

Fan-shaped cut

Rhizome

2. With a sharp knife, cut the rhizomes into sections. Each section must have healthy leaves and roots attached.

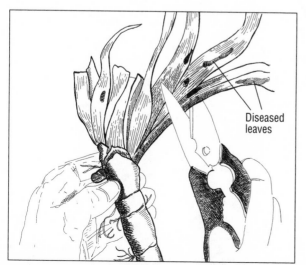

Diseased leaves

3. Cut the leaves into 5-inch fan shapes with garden shears or kitchen scissors. Cut off any diseased or discolored growth and discard.

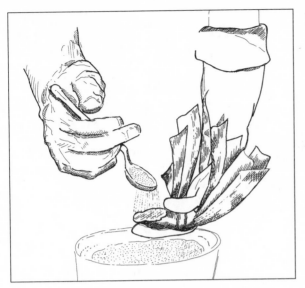

4. Dip iris divisions in a bucket of water containing 1 cup of liquid bleach before transplanting to kill any unseen borer larvae.

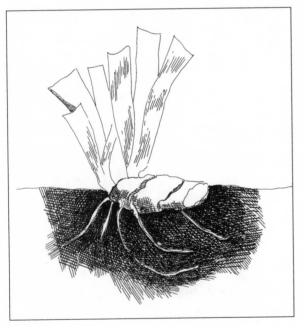

5. Transplant the new divisions 12 to 18 inches apart. The rhizomes should be half in and half out of the soil, with roots firmed into place. Irises like to be baked by the sun.

Dividing Peonies

Divide peonies in the fall as follows.

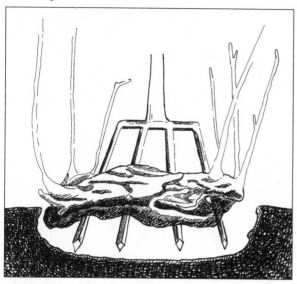

1. Use a garden fork to lift the roots, taking care not to break them.

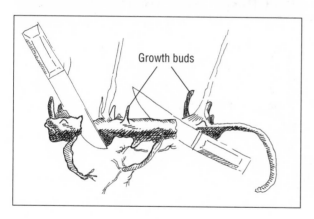

Growth buds

2. With a sharp knife, cut the large, fleshy roots into pieces. each piece containing three to five eyes (prominent red growth buds). Wash the divisions clean.

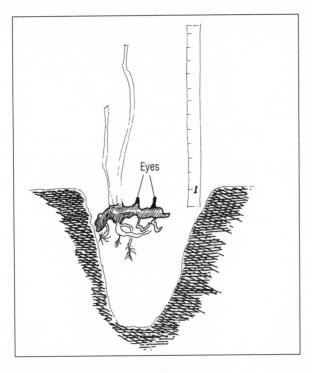

3. Plant the cut sections in new locations 12 to 18 inches apart. The eyes must be no more than 1 inch below the soil surface or the plant will produce only foliage—no blooms. Use a ruler to be sure. Add or remove soil to achieve the proper depth as you water in the new divisions.

Dividing Perennials with Taproots That Resent Disturbance

1. Prepare new holes first, digging wide enough and deep enough (approximately 18 inches) to accommodate the taproots at the same depth they were growing before division.

2. Dig deeply around the plant—18 inches or so—to get as much root as possible.

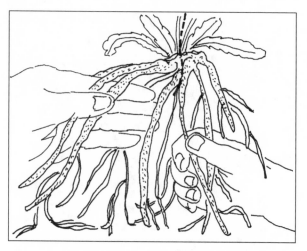

3. Lift the clump out of the ground and gently pull apart the thonglike roots. Divide them into pieces containing one to three crowns.

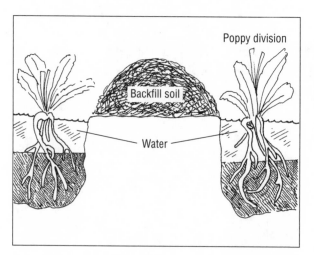

Poppy division

Backfill soil

Water

4. Place the divisions in the new holes, and shovel soil to the halfway mark around each one. Pour water to fill the holes. This will settle soil among the roots and ensure that they are adequately moist.

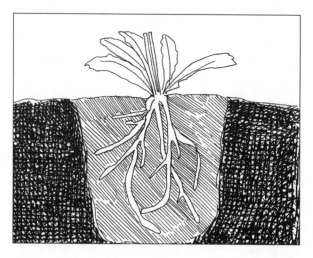

5. When the water has drained away, use the remaining soil to fill the holes.

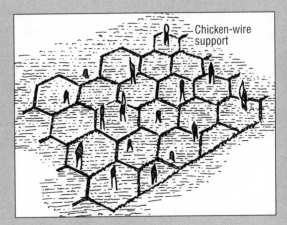

Chicken-wire support

To ensure that blooming-size peonies are not flattened by spring rains and wind, place a piece of chicken wire, cut to match the size of the planting, flat on the ground before the new shoots appear in the spring. The new growth will lift the wire 10 to 12 inches above the ground. Each stem will have its own support, and the clump will stand erect. No string or stakes are required. The new foliage will hide the chicken wire from view. In the late fall, remove the wire when you trim and clean up the flower beds.

Planting and Transplanting

9

Planting Bulbs

ॐ

THE TERM *BULB* IS LOOSELY APPLIED to any plant that has a thick basal portion. There are true bulbs (daffodils), corms (gladioli), rhizomes (iris), tubers (tuberous begonias), and tuberous roots (cannas). All have one thing in common: They are food storage containers from which the plant can prepare for next season's bloom after a dormant season. Although we usually think of bulbs as spring bloomers, different varieties of bulbs can be planted for continuous bloom throughout the growing season, depending on climate. If properly cultivated, allowed to ripen after blooming, and given a warm, dry resting period, bulbs can provide flowers for the garden and the home throughout the year.

The following are some favorite spring and summer flowering bulbs:

Calla lily *(Zantedeschia aethiopica)*. Rhizome. Flowers: pink, white, yellow. Planting time: spring or fall. Planting depth: 2 to 6 inches (depending on size of rhizome, variety, and climate). Spacing: 1 to 2 feet.

Crocus (*Crocus* spp.). Corm. Flowers: yellow, orange, white, blue, purple. Planting time: fall. Planting depth: 2 to 3 inches. Spacing: 4 inches.

Grape hyacinth (*Muscari spp.*). True bulb. Flowers: blue, white. Planting time: fall. Planting depth: 2 inches. Spacing: 2 to 4 inches.

Hyacinth *(Hyacinthus orientalis)*. True bulb. Flowers: red, pink, blue, purple, white. Planting time: fall. Planting depth: 4 to 6 inches. Spacing: 6 to 8 inches.

Iris (*Iris* spp.). Rhizome or true bulb. Flowers: many colors; some bicolored. Planting time: fall. Planting depth: bulbs, 4 inches; rhizomes, tops just beneath the soil surface. Spacing: bulbs, 3 to 4 inches; rhizomes, 1 foot apart.

Lily (*Lilium* spp.). True bulb. Flowers: many colors; some bicolored. Planting time: fall. Planting depth: 3 to 5 inches. Spacing: 6 to 12 inches.

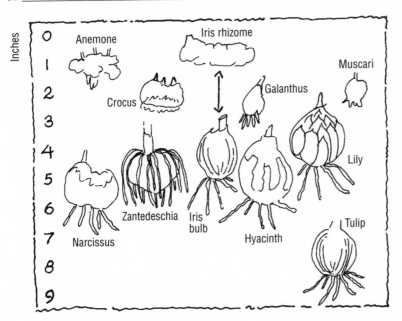

Narcissus (*Narcissus* spp.). True bulb. Flowers: yellow, orange, white; some bicolored. Planting time: fall. Planting depth: 3 to 6 inches (depending on size of bulb—the larger, the deeper). Spacing: 3 to 8 inches.

Snowdrop (*Galanthus* spp.). True bulb. Flowers: white. Planting time: fall. Planting depth: 2 to 3 inches. Spacing: 2 to 4 inches.

Tulip (*Tulipa* spp.). True bulb. Flowers: many colors; some bicolored. Planting time: fall. Planting depth: 6 to 8 inches (depending on size of bulb). Spacing: 4 to 8 inches.

Windflower (*Anemone* spp.). Tuberous root. Flowers: blue, red, pink, white. Planting time: fall. Planting depth: 1 inch. Spacing: 6 inches.

TOOLS AND SUPPLIES

Round-pointed shovel
Trowel
Rake
Wheelbarrow

Compost, leaf mulch, or sphagnum peat moss
Commercial bulb food or 5–10–5 fertilizer
Labels

Planting Bulbs in Small Areas

You don't need to plant hundreds of bulbs for them to light up your garden. A few handfuls planted in odd numbers here and there are surprisingly effective and spiritually uplifting, especially when the surrounding landscape is still recovering from the effects of winter. Plant them in areas you pass frequently—by the back porch steps, along the driveway, under a favorite tree. Try for a natural effect—little clusters scattered about—to catch the eye. Plant them where they will get full sun or just a little light shade.

1. Using a round-pointed shovel, dig a flowerpot-shaped hole 1 foot in diameter and 7 inches deep. A hole this size should accommodate 11 average-size tulip bulbs. Vary the hole diameter and depth according to the size of the bulbs you are planting.

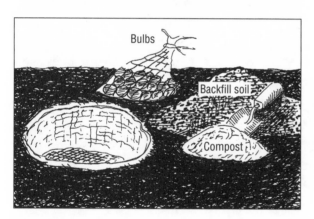

2. Mix the backfill soil (the dug-up soil that will go back into the planting hole) with two or three trowelfuls of compost, sphagnum peat moss, or leaf mulch. Remove any stones.

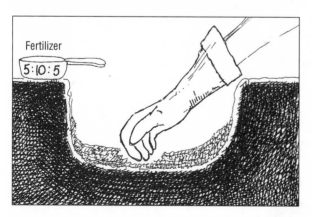

3. Using your hands or a trowel, mix 1/2 cup of 5-10-5 fertilizer or bulb food into the soil in the bottom of each hole. If your holes are smaller or larger than 1 foot by 7 inches, vary the amount of fertilizer accordingly.

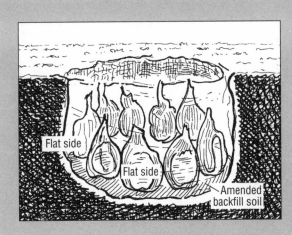

When planting tulips in a cluster, place the flat side of each bulb facing out and the round side facing in. This way, when the bulbs are in bloom, a fan of leaves will surround the clump for a bouquetlike appearance. Plant the bulbs with growing tips up, 6 to 8 inches deep, 4 to 8 inches apart.

4. Fill the hole with the amended backfill soil, and firm into place by hand. Water thoroughly. Label bulb plantings, or make a drawing of your beds with each planting carefully identified.

Planting Bulbs in Large Beds

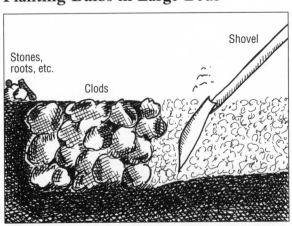

1. With a shovel, turn the soil to a depth of 9 to 12 inches. Break up the clods as you turn over each shovelful. Remove old roots, stones, and weeds as you dig.

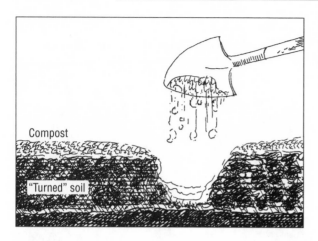

2. Spread organic matter such as compost, leaf mulch, or sphagnum peat moss to a depth of 3 inches over the freshly dug bed. Use your shovel to work this in.

3. Scatter 5–10–5 fertilizer or bulb food at the rate of 3/4 pound per 25 square feet. Work it into the bed, then rake smooth.

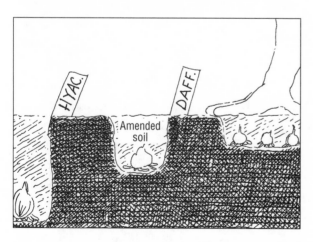

4. Using a trowel, dig individual holes for your bulbs, spaced according to the bulb chart. Plant the bulbs with the growing end up, cover them with amended soil, and firm into place with your hands. Water well.

Forcing Bulbs in Containers

Forcing means stimulating bulbs to flower out of season. Ask at a garden center which varieties are best for forcing.

TOOLS AND SUPPLIES

Containers for forcing (at least 6 inches deep, and large enough to hold six daffodil bulbs)
Stones or gravel

Commercial potting mix, or perlite and garden soil
Baking pan
Pea gravel

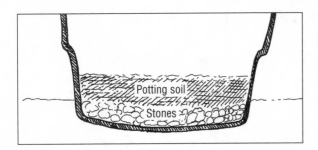

1. Place 1 inch of stones or gravel in the bottom of your container for drainage. Fill the container with 2 inches of professional potting mix or an equal blend of garden soil and perlite.

2. Place the bulbs in the container so that they are almost touching, and fill with soil. The mix should be 1/2 inch from the rim of the container, with the tips of the bulbs showing. Water well.

3. Store the potted bulbs in a dark, cool location such as an unheated garage, cool attic, or basement. Your location shouldn't be any warmer than 50 degrees, nor should it freeze. If your storage location is cool, it is not necessary to water the bulbs during this period. After twelve weeks, check on growth.

4. When shoots have appeared, bring the pots into a bright, well-lighted room. Do not place the containers in direct sunlight. Place the pots on a baking pan filled with pea gravel, and water thoroughly. Do not overwater; pots should never be soggy.

5. When shoots are 5 to 6 inches tall, place your containers in a sunny location, and wait for them to bloom.

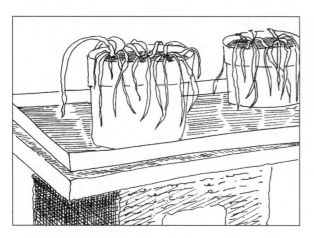

6. After the flowers fade, return the pots to a cool location and do not water. Allow the foliage to die down gradually—don't cut it back—and transplant the bulbs in the garden in late spring.

Tips for Gardening with Bulbs

• When buying bulbs, look for the largest and firmest ones; these always produce the best blooms, and are worth the extra expense.

• Never cut off bulb foliage until it has ripened, or died back naturally, usually about six weeks after blooming has stopped. The ripening foliage provides nutrients that are stored in the bulb for the next season's bloom.

• Cut off spent blooms of spring and summer flowering bulbs. Seedpod formation robs the bulb of energy. This is especially important with tulips, daffodils, and hyacinths.

• Do not use manure when planting bulbs. It may cause botrytis blight (blasting of the buds). Use only a balanced fertilizer, bone meal, or bulb food.

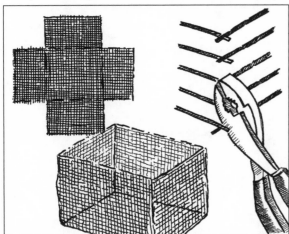

• If you have trouble with rodents, construct cages out of 1/2-inch wire mesh.

Dig the area to the correct bulb-planting depth, and sink cages in the ground. Fill with soil, and plant your bulbs within the cage. This can be a tedious process if you plant large numbers of bulbs, but it works.

S tand cut daffodils in a bucket of water for three hours before mixing them with other flowers in an arrangement. Daffodils exude a slimy substance that is toxic to irises, roses, and hyacinths. After three hours, the substance dissipates and they are safe to use.

- If your bulbs are dug out of the ground by dogs looking for bones or skunks searching for grubs, use superphosphate instead of bone meal as a fertilizer.
- Failure to bloom may be due to overcrowding. Dig, separate, and replant your bulbs every three years in the late spring after the foliage has ripened.
- Some gardeners like to soak bulbs in liquid fertilizer for an hour before planting. If you do this, avoid fish emulsion fertilizers, which attract raccoons.
- Never allow lily bulbs to dry out. If you cannot plant them immediately, be sure to mist the bulbs to keep them damp, but not soaked, until you get them into the ground.

10

Transplanting Young Stock

❧

MANY GARDENERS PURCHASE YOUNG PLANTS from nurseries rather than starting their own from seed. Although most plants can be grown from seed, some perennials, such as bleeding hearts, asters, and astilbes, are easier to establish if purchased already growing in containers. And if you experience a sudden loss when growing your own plants from seed, annual bedding stock is readily available at garden centers to fill in the gaps. Always buy plants from a reputable nursery. If you have just moved into a new neighborhood, ask around.

Buy container-grown plants early in the season to avoid root-bound stock. Avoid plants with thick masses of roots on the soil surface or protruding from drainage holes; they will have more difficulty establishing a normal root system when transplanted. Girdling roots—those tightly wrapped around the stem or protruding from burlap—restrict healthy growth once planted. Managers of garden centers may frown on your poking around to check on root growth, but this inspection can be done unobtrusively, especially with plants in cell packs.

April to May is the best time to transplant in mild climates. Prepare your beds when the soil is crumbly. Daytime temperatures should average 60 to 80 degrees F., and nighttime 40 to 50 degrees F.

TOOLS AND SUPPLIES

Knife	Gloves
Trowel or putty-knife	Mulch
Shovel or spade	

Transplanting from Flats

1. Dig generous holes in the garden bed, large enough to accommodate the root balls. Space the holes according to the directions on the plant label.

2. Water the flat to moisten the soil before you remove the plants. With a putty knife, trowel, or similar tool, cut straight down around each plant, and lift it out as if you were using a spatula.

3. If roots are matted and intertwined, carefully pull them apart so that most of the roots remain intact.

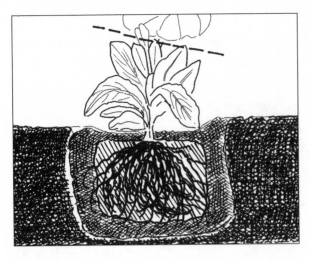

4. Set each plant in its hole so that the root ball is slightly lower than it was in the flat. Backfill around the plant with loose, friable soil. Firm the soil by hand. Pinch off buds and flowers so that the plant's energy can be used to establish roots. Water gently and thoroughly.

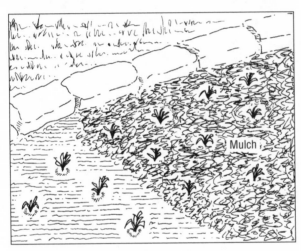

5. Mulch the entire area containing the transplants with 1 inch of compost, well-rotted sawdust or manure, pine needles, pine bark chips, or other mulch to conserve soil moisture and to maintain an even temperature. Tuck the mulch evenly around the stems of each new transplant.

6. If the sunlight is intense, shade the new transplants with bushel baskets, newspaper tents, or cardboard boxes.

Transplanting from Cell Packs

1. Poke a finger under the bottom of each plastic cell and push the plants while lifting them out.

2. Separate the plants, carefully teasing the roots apart. Follow steps 4 through 6 for Transplanting from Flats, above.

Transplanting from Pots

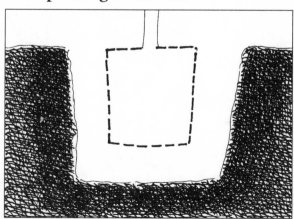

1. Prepare a hole for the plant that is 50 percent larger than the container.

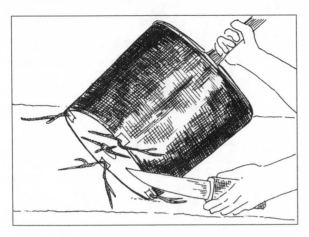

2. Before you remove the plant, moisten the soil, and use a sharp knife to trim off any roots protruding from the drainage holes to facilitate removal.

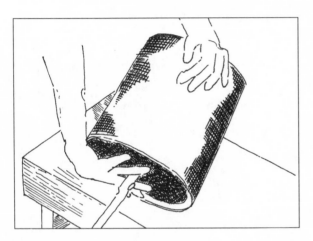

3. Place one hand on top of the pot, with the stem of the plant between your index and middle fingers. Grasp the pot with your other hand, invert it, then gently pull it off while steadying the root ball. If the plant is root-bound, you may first need to tap the rim of the pot on a hard surface to loosen the plant.

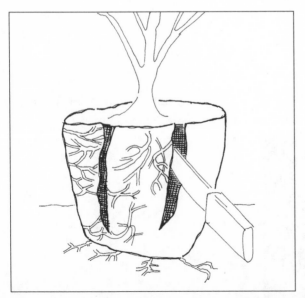

4. If the roots are crowded and matted, use a sharp knife to score the sides of the root ball from top to bottom 1/8 to 1/4 inch deep. Score every 3 inches around the root ball, and loosen the roots in the bottom with the knife.

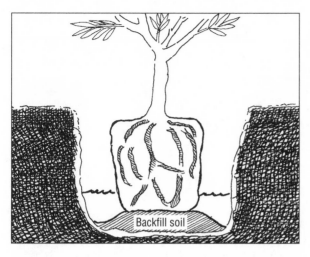

5. Position the plant in the hole so that it is at the same level as it was in the container. To achieve the correct depth, add backfill soil to the bottom of the hole first, then add or subtract as necessary. Water the plant thoroughly.

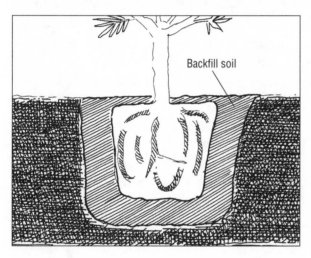

6. After the water drains away, fill around the root ball with soil to the top of the hole, and firm it into place.

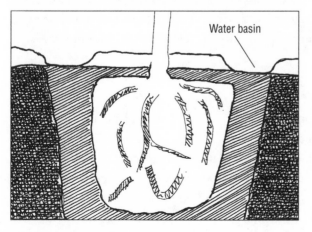

7. Water again, then mulch as in step 5 of Transplanting from Flats, above.

11

Planting Trees

୫ଧ

SELECTING A TREE FOR YOUR PROPERTY demands thought. How do you want the tree to serve you? Will it provide shade, function as a screen or windbreak, provide food for the birds? Do you want an evergreen or a deciduous tree? What are the tree's cultural requirements, winter hardiness, ultimate height and spread? Will the tree fit in with your other plantings and the surrounding environment? If you have a sentimental attachment to a particular type of tree from your childhood—and many people do—will this variety be suitable for your house and garden? You must pick the right tree for the right place.

Once you decide on the type of tree, you can buy it bare-root, container-grown, or balled-and-burlapped. Bare-root trees are available from mail-order nurseries, your local county conservation district headquarters, the Bureau of Forestry, and some garden centers. Mail-order nurseries often guarantee their stock and grow their own plants. They are good sources for rare and unusual plants that cannot always be found at the local garden center. Many mail-order nurseries ship their plants during the dormant season. These trees are generally inexpensive, allowing you to purchase quantities of trees for planting large areas.

Many varieties of trees are sold in containers made of peat fiber, plastic, or wood. Trees usually come in 10- and 15-gallon containers, but specimen trees are often sold in wooden boxes.

Balled-and-burlapped (B&B) trees are raised in the field, then dug up and the root balls wrapped in burlap. In severe winter climates, many different varieties of trees are sold balled-and-burlapped because they are less susceptible to winter freezing than plants in containers.

Trees purchased in containers and balled-and-burlapped trees can be planted whenever the soil can be worked. In the North, the best times for planting bare-root deciduous trees are in early spring or late fall while plants are dormant. Bare-root needleleaf evergreens should be planted in spring because they need the moisture supplied by frequent rainfall and are less likely to suffer from dehydration. In the South, winter is a perfect time for planting trees.

Consider the planting of a tree as a long-term investment. Look for a straight trunk, a well-balanced system of branches, and good leaf color. Avoid plants with nicks or cuts in the bark or circling roots at the top of the container. Never buy a B&B or container-grown tree that is wilted; it may not recover. Check the foliage before you buy. Yellowed leaves or signs of pests indicate a stressed plant. Beware of bargain prices.

Trees do best in the company of other trees, but if you must plant a single specimen in the center of the lawn, amend the soil at planting time, water it during dry spells, and mulch it heavily to keep the roots cool.

TOOLS AND SUPPLIES

Spade or shovel	Mulch
Pruning shears	Soil amendments (sphagnum peat moss, leaf mulch, compost)
Tin snips	Wood stakes
Sharp knife	

Planting Bare-root Trees

Bare-root trees are usually ordered by mail and shipped in a dormant state. Nurseries will send them at the correct planting time for your region or at the date you request. Order early enough to get what you want at the right time. You may also find bare-root stock locally.

1. If you can plant the tree on its arrival, first unwrap it and soak the roots in a bucket of water for two or three hours. If you cannot plant for three or four days, unwrap the tree and cover the roots with wet newspaper, burlap, or cloth. Store it in a cool place such as a garage or basement. Soak the roots in a bucket of water for two to three hours before planting.

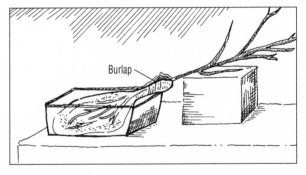

If you must wait several weeks to plant, dig a trench in a sheltered location deep enough to accommodate all the roots without crowding. This technique is called heeling-in. Lay the trunk against the edge of the trench for support. Cover the roots with soil, and round off the top. After heeling-in, water the roots thoroughly once a week until you can plant the tree in its permanent location. It will not be necessary to soak the tree roots before planting.

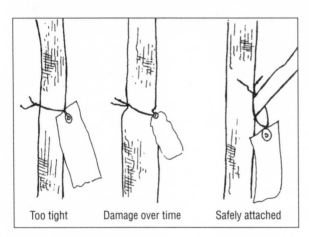

Too tight   Damage over time   Safely attached

2. If the tree arrives with a wired label, remove it or—if you need to keep the tree labeled—reattach it to a smaller side branch. Otherwise, the wire may severely damage the trunk as the tree grows.

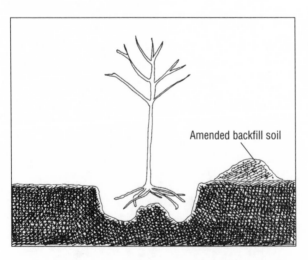

Amended backfill soil

3. When you are ready to plant, dig a hole large enough to accommodate all the roots without bending them. Amend the backfill soil with generous amounts of organic material, such as compost, leaf mulch, or sphagnum peat moss.

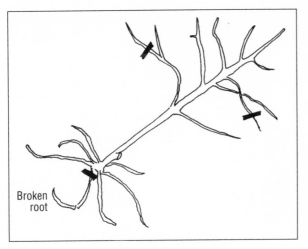

4. Prune off any broken or damaged roots and branches. If the tree has more branches than you think the root system can support, prune 3 to 4 inches off the ends of the branches.

Broken root

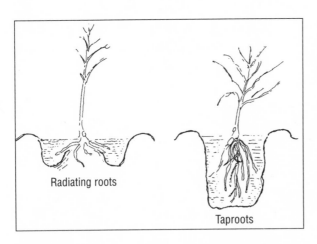

Radiating roots

Taproots

5. If the roots radiate in a circle, make a cone-shaped mound by hand from amended backfill soil, and spread the roots over this mound. If the tree has a taproot (common with fruit trees), this is not necessary.

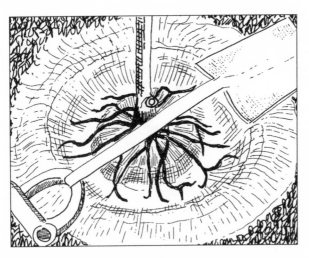

6. Use the handle of a shovel or spade as a guideline to set the tree at the correct level. The tree should be planted at the same depth at which it was originally grown. This can usually be determined from the soil mark on the bark. If you can't determine the original soil line, position the top root 1 inch below the surface unless the tree is budded or grafted, indicated by a knobby joint at the base of the trunk. In that case, position the joint 2 inches above the soil surface.

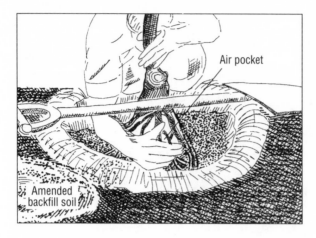

7. Using your hands, work the amended soil between the roots, and try to fill any air pockets. Keep the trunk straight, and do not remove the handle of the spade until you have filled the hole with soil, firmed it into place, and watered the tree. This job often requires two people.

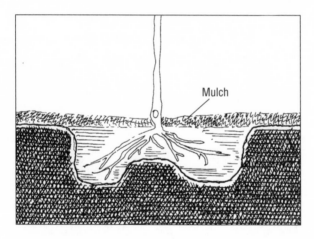

8. Mulch around the tree above the soil level 3 to 4 inches deep with pine bark chips, pine needles, or similar organic material to conserve moisture.

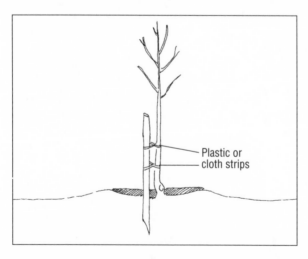

9. Most bare-root trees are small and don't need staking the first year. But if you feel your tree may suffer from wind damage, drive a stake at least twice as thick as the trunk 18 inches into the ground next to the tree. The stake should stand one-half the height of the tree. Tie the tree to the stake with two or three strips of plastic or cloth. Do not use wire.

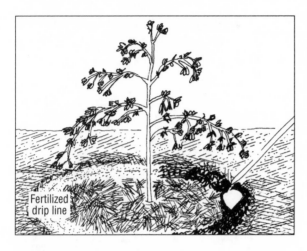

10. Fertilize when leaves appear in the spring and not before. Sprinkle 2 cups of all-purpose 5–10–5 fertilizer around the plant at the drip line. Hoe it into the soil, and water well.

Fertilized drip line

Planting Container-grown Trees

Nurseries often sell trees in 5- to 15-gallon plastic pots, peach baskets, or peat fiber pots. They cost more than bare-root stock but are cheaper than balled-and-burlapped.

Amendments

Backfill soil

1. Dig the hole for the tree 50 percent larger than its container. Amend the backfill soil with generous quantities of damp sphagnum peat moss, leaf mulch, or compost.

2. Water the tree while it is still in the container; the soil should be moist before you remove the tree.

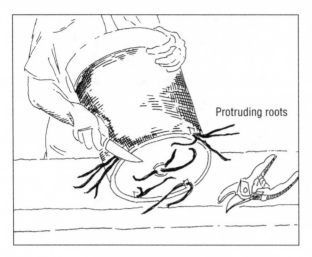

3. Using pruning shears or a knife, cut away any roots protruding from drainage holes.

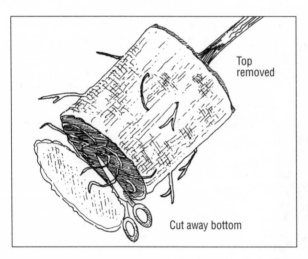

4. If the tree is in a plastic pot, gently pull off the pot if possible. If not, use tin snips to cut from top to bottom down opposite sides. Do not crumble the root ball. If the tree is in a peach basket or fiber pot, cut away the bottom of the container with tin snips, and plant the entire container. The basket or peat fiber will disintegrate quickly. Cut off the top of a peatfiber pot so that it is even with the soil in the container. If the fiber is exposed, it will draw moisture away from the plant.

5. For trees that have been removed from the container, use a knife to loosen large roots encircling the root ball. If you fail to do so, the tree's growth may be stunted.

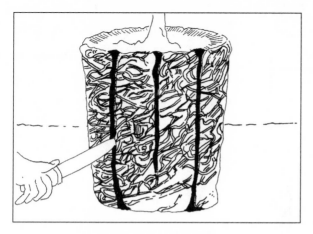

6. Tease apart smaller roots. If they are severely matted, score the sides with a sharp knife, making cuts 1/8 to 1/4 inch deep from top to bottom. Score every 3 inches around the root ball.

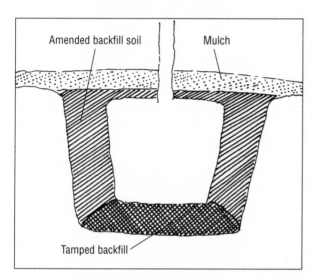

Amended backfill soil

Mulch

Tamped backfill

7. Place the tree in the hole, and adjust the root ball so that the tree will rest no higher than it was growing in the container. Fill around the sides of the hole with amended backfill soil, tamp down firmly around the entire root ball, level off, and water thoroughly. Mulch around the tree above the soil level 3 to 4 inches deep with pine bark chips, pine needles, or similar organic material. Fertilize the tree only if you are planting in the spring. Fall fertilizing encourages soft growth that may suffer severe winter dieback.

Planting Balled-and-burlapped (B&B) Trees

When you select a B&B tree, make certain the ball is solid and shows no sign of having crumbled. Move a B&B tree from the bottom of the root ball; never use the trunk as a handle. The best time to plant B&B trees is late fall, but many can be planted safely in the spring.

1. If you can't plant a B&B tree immediately, stand it in the shade, cover the burlap with straw or plastic to maintain moisture, and keep the burlap and foliage moist.

2. When you're ready to plant, dig a hole no deeper than the root ball but twice as wide. Amend the backfill soil with generous quantities of damp sphagnum peat moss, leaf mulch, or compost.

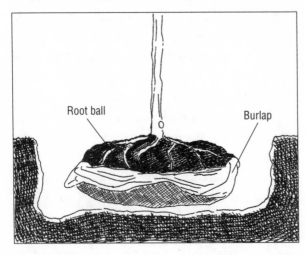

Root ball

Burlap

3. Gently lower the root ball into the hole. The tree should be at the same depth at which it was growing in the field. Untie the string surrounding the base of the trunk. Pull back the burlap 6 to 8 inches, and flatten it down against the root ball.

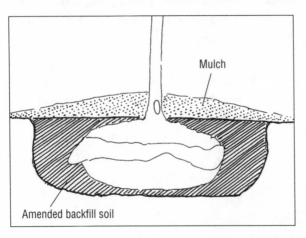

Mulch

Amended backfill soil

4. Fill the space around the root ball with amended backfill soil, being sure to cover the edges of the burlap with soil; exposed burlap will draw moisture away from the root ball. Tamp down, and water thoroughly. Mulch 3 to 4 inches deep around the base of the tree. Fertilize B&B trees in the spring, as in step 10 for Planting Bare-root Trees, above.

12

Moving a Small Tree or Shrub

෫ඁ

YOU WANT TO BUILD an addition to your home, right where the cherry tree is, or a valuable shrub is struggling to survive in full sun and needs more shade. Can you move it?

Transplanting is worth trying if the tree is no more than 6 feet tall, the shrub no more than 3. Before you move it, though, check a garden reference source for its ultimate size. Will it fit into the new site five years hence? Does it require full sun or partial shade for best growth? Select a spot as carefully as you would for a new plant.

The best time for moving small trees and shrubs is late fall, about six weeks before the first hard freeze. This will allow some root growth to begin. You can also move them in early spring before branches leaf out. If you are in doubt about transplanting a tree or shrub because of its size, talk to an experienced nursery owner.

TOOLS AND SUPPLIES

Shovel or spade

Tree wrap

Mulch

Compost and other soil amendments

Knife or garden scissors

Heavy twine

Burlap sacking

1. Some shrubs can be pruned to ground level before moving. Do this first if possible, following the guidelines in chapter 16.

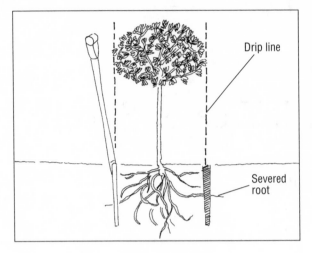

Drip line

Severed root

2. Cut the outer roots two weeks before transplanting by sinking a shovel its full depth in a circle around the drip line— the circumference of the plant formed by the outer tips of the branches. The plant will adjust to the shock and will begin forming new feeder roots closer to the main stem.

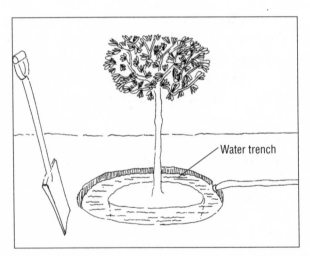

Water trench

3. Two or three days before you move the plant, use a shovel to make a trench 4 or 5 inches deep around the entire drip line. Slowly fill the trench with water, allowing it to permeate the soil around the root zone.

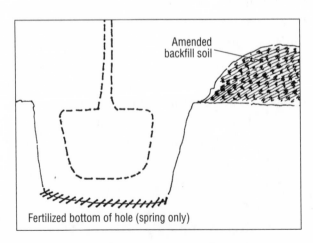

Amended backfill soil

Fertilized bottom of hole (spring only)

4. Prepare the new hole before you move the tree or shrub. It should be 50 percent larger than the size of the root ball. Amend the backfill soil with compost, damp sphagnum peat moss, leaf mulch, or other soil amendments. If you transplant in the spring, sprinkle 1 cup of all-purpose fertilizer (5–10–5) in the bottom of the new hole. Blend it into the soil.

5. Cut down with a spade or the back of a shovel to form the root ball. Heavy, clay soil holds together well, allowing for a larger root ball. Large root balls can, however, be very heavy. Try to make the size manageable. The size of a bushel basket should be adequate.

6. Using a shovel, cut down the sides of the hole and remove the soil to provide space for wrapping. Cut one half way under the root ball on one side. Try not to crumble the soil.

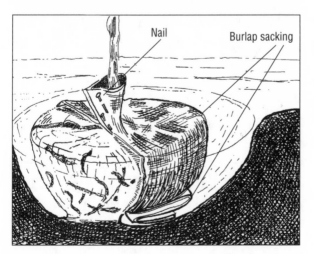

Nail Burlap sacking

7. Place burlap sacking underneath the cut half, and pull it up to the base of the trunk. Pin the overlapped sacking together around the base of the trunk with nails, as though pinning pieces of cloth together.

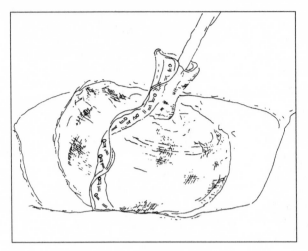

8. Continue the digging process around the other half of the root ball. Pull the sacking under the plant and upward until the entire root ball is covered. Secure it tightly on all sides, and pin the top, around the base of the trunk, with nails. The sacking should fit as tightly as the skin on an onion.

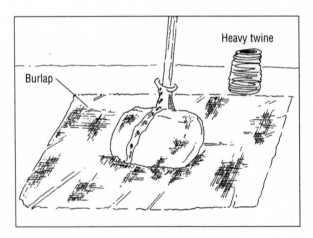

9. Gently lift the plant out, and place it on a square of burlap large enough for a second wrapping. Try not to loosen the soil around the root ball.

10. Pin the second layer of burlap sacking with nails, and then surround it with heavy twine by wrapping first around the base, then upward to secure the entire root ball. Tie the twine several times, and pull it tightly around the root ball to prevent the burlap from slipping as you move the plant to its new location. Lift by root ball, not trunk. This may take several people. Do not break the root ball.

11. Gently lower the plant into the new hole, positioning it at the same level it was growing previously.

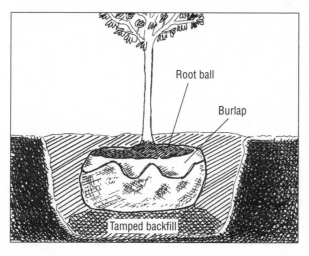

Root ball

Burlap

Tamped backfill

12. Untie the twine from around the burlap, remove the nails, and fold back all burlap sacking 6 to 8 inches from the trunk. It should lie against the sides of the root ball. Fill around the sides of the root ball with amended soil, and pack it in so that the plant is firmly anchored. Cover the burlap entirely; it will gradually rot as the plant grows. Slowly water until the entire root ball has been saturated. Repeat this process once a week for a month if the weather is dry.

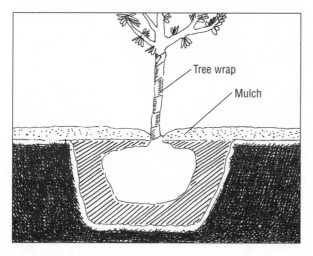

Tree wrap

Mulch

13. Mulch the newly planted tree or shrub with pine bark chips or another organic material to conserve moisture. Wrap the trunk of a newly planted tree from its base to the first set of branches with tree wrap to guard against sunscald and to deter rodents and deer.

Cultivation

13

Hoeing, Cultivating, and Weeding

&

ONE OF THE MOST USEFUL TOOLS in the gardener's armory is the basic garden hoe, a tool that has been employed for more than 4000 years. You can use it to uproot weeds, till the soil to allow moisture and air to get in, or make a furrow for planting seeds. Handled properly, a garden hoe can weed and cultivate at the same time.

Garden centers and hardware stores carry a wide assortment of tools labeled hoes or cultivators that are used to wage war against weeds. Small hand tools for kneeling or sitting jobs have business ends like the regular-size tools, but with palm-size handles. Some hoes have 2 1/2-inch-wide blades for light jobs in narrow spots; others have 8-inch-wide blades for drives and walks. If you invest in only one hoe, however, get the basic long-handled garden hoe with a 6-inch-wide blade.

TOOLS AND SUPPLIES

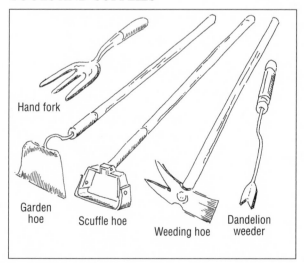

Hand fork

Garden hoe

Scuffle hoe

Weeding hoe

Dandelion weeder

Long-handled garden hoe with a 6-inch blade
File
Long-handled scuffle hoe or Dutch hoe (optional)
Long-handled weeding hoe (optional)
Hand fork (optional)
Dandelion weeder (optional)

The Basic Garden Hoe

The basic garden hoe can perform a multitude of jobs. You can use it to push soil up and around a plant or pull it away. By holding the blade at an angle, you can make furrows for planting seeds. You can chop the soil to a depth of 1¹/2 inches, exposing the weeds (tops and roots) so that the sun will kill them. At the same time, you are aerating the soil and allowing moisture to reach plant roots.

If you hoe properly, you will dig up very little soil. Most vegetable crops have shallow roots, so hoe 4 to 6 inches away from the rows or individual plants. Walk backward to avoid treading on uprooted weeds, thereby rerooting them. The job is easier if the ground is moist, but not muddy. If the weather is wet, rake up the weeds you have hoed to prevent rerooting.

The Scuffle Hoe and Dutch Hoe

The scuffle hoe and Dutch hoe are used for weeding only; they are not used for cultivating the soil or for making hills and furrows. They destroy weeds easily because the blades are sharp on both sides. The scuffle hoe comes with an oscillating blade that chops at the angle you want as you change direction. The Dutch hoe does not oscillate.

Don't chop, but push the hoe ahead of you as if you were playing shuffleboard. It will cut off the weed stems just below the surface of the soil. Both types of hoes are efficient tools for fast, easy removal of weeds.

The Weeding Hoe

The weeding hoe has a blade on one side for hoeing and a forked weed puller on the other. Its basic advantage is that if you have persistent perennial weeds in your garden, you can use the forked end to uproot them, saving you from having to stoop down to remove them with a hand tool.

The Hand Fork

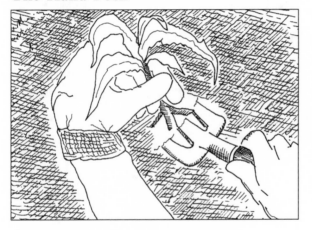

The hand fork is a pronged tool that is useful for working in small places around plants, but you must kneel or sit on the ground to use it effectively. Use it to kill weeds by chopping the soil, cutting off mature weeds, and digging out roots. Be cautious; you may damage a prize plant if you are careless.

The Dandelion Weeder

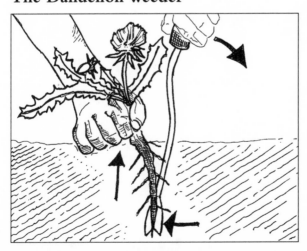

Dandelions have long taproots, and if the entire root is not removed, the plant will regenerate. This tool, with its long, thin blade and notched tip, is designed to get the whole taproot out.

Sink the tool along the exact line of the taproot—take good aim and be precise. Wiggle it around the taproot, loosen the plant, and pull the plant out with the forked tip.

Sharpening a Hoe

A hoe is a cutting tool and must be kept sharp. Sharpen your hoe every few hours when in use, especially if your soil is gravelly.

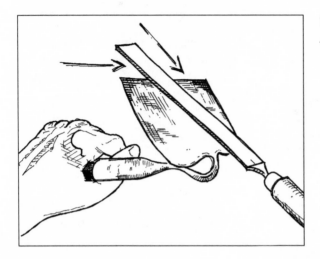

1. File the slanted side of the blade at a 45-degree angle.

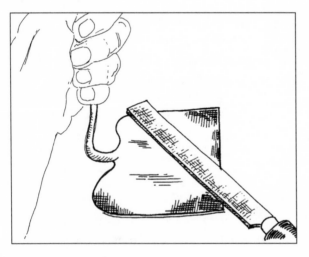

2. Smooth the back by briskly rubbing the file flat against it to remove any rough spots.

Weeds to Watch Out For

Weeds with Taproots

Dandelion *(Taraxacum officinale)*

Docks (*Rumex* spp.)

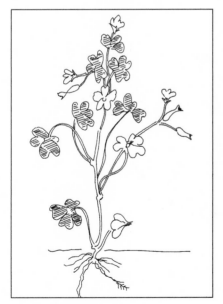

Oxalis *(Oxalis stricta)*

Plantain (*Plantago* spp.)

Underground Creepers

Ground elder *(Aegopodium podagraria)*

Bindweed *(Convolvulus arvensis)*

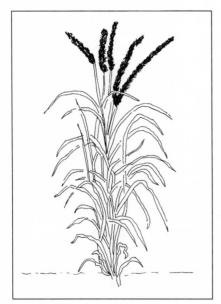

Couch grass *(Agropyron repens)*

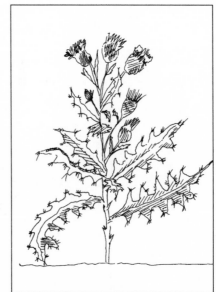

Canada thistle *(Cirsium arvense)*

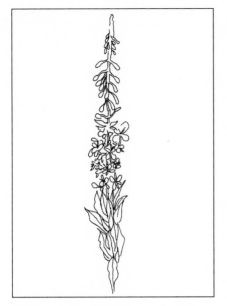

Rosebay willow-herb *(Epilobium angustifolium)*

Japanese knotweed *(Polygonum cuspidatum)*

Surface Creepers

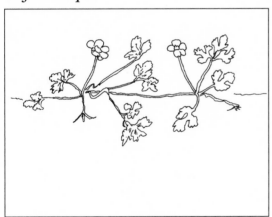

Creeping buttercup *(Ranunculus repens)*

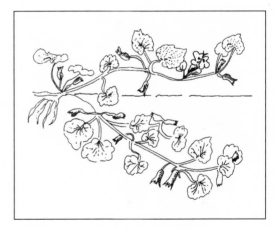

Ground ivy *(Glechoma hederacea)*

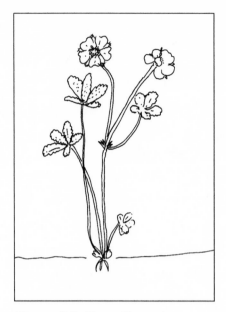

Cinquefoil (*Potentilla* spp.)

Weeds That Spread by Seed

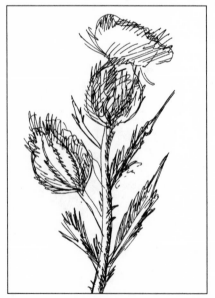

Bull thistle *(Cirsium vulgare)*

14

Mulching

MULCHING IS COVERING THE SURFACE of the soil with a layer of organic or inorganic material. This should be done after the soil has warmed up in the spring. Mulches cut down on work and contribute to your plants' health by retarding weed growth, preserving soil moisture, reducing soil temperature extremes, and preventing heaving of plants from winter freezing and thawing. Organic mulches improve soil fertility by adding humus as the bottom layers break down, and they reduce the spread of diseases. Your success as a gardener depends on mulching.

Mulching materials include black plastic, brown paper, newspaper, peat moss and compost, shredded or chipped bark, sawdust, pine needles, straw or hay, dead leaves, dried grass clippings, and crushed rock or stone chips. Different mulches serve different purposes. In the ornamental garden, an attractive organic mulch enhances the appearance of your plantings; in the vegetable garden, black plastic is ideal.

Black Plastic

Black plastic is the most effective mulch for eradicating perennial weeds, because it shuts out light needed by weeds for germination. Thus it is an excellent mulch for the vegetable garden. It warms up the soil and maintains even moisture throughout the bed, making it ideal for strawberries, cabbages, Brussels sprouts, and squash. It is not attractive in ornamental gardens, but if you wish to use it there, you can cover it with an organic mulch.

To calculate the required volume of mulch in cubic feet, multiply its depth in inches by the soil area in square feet, and divide by 12.

1. Before laying black plastic, anticipate where you will place and space your plants. Cultivate the soil between rows, and mound it slightly around and between the spots where you will insert plants so that water will run toward the base of the plants.

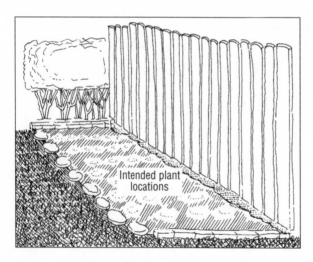

2. After cultivating and before planting, spread the plastic. Anchor the sides of the plastic with stones or bury the edges with a few shovelfuls of soil so that the wind will not blow it.

3. Cut cross-slits with a knife where you intend to insert young plants. A 3-inch slit is adequate for most plants. Slash more 3-inch slits along the rows so that water can enter, or lay a soaker hose under the plastic.

Brown Paper and Biodegradable Plastic

Brown paper and biodegradable plastic are sold as mulches. Brown paper is preferable to biodegradable plastic because it decomposes completely; biodegradable plastic does not, and you will wind up with strips blowing about the garden. Brown paper is not unattractive in a flower border; you also may cover it with organic mulch.

The procedure for laying brown paper and biodegradable plastic is the same as for black plastic. Brown paper mulch used for ornamental plantings may be worked into the soil at the end of the season.

Newspaper

Newspaper is an inexpensive mulch for vegetable gardens and flower borders, but applying it is time-consuming. Avoid using glossy or colored sheets, which contain chemicals that may be harmful to the soil. Lay six sheets at a time, following the procedure for laying black plastic. Newspapers have a tendency to dry out quickly, so cover them with organic mulch. Newspapers may be cultivated into the soil at the end of the season or after harvesting.

Peat Moss and Compost

Peat moss and compost applied in layers makes an attractive, organically rich, mulch for any garden area. A mixture is best, because pure peat moss tends to form a crust that sheds water away from plant roots. Peat and compost contribute much-needed humus to the soil, moderate soil temperatures throughout the growing season, and allow moisture to reach plant roots easily. Spread this mulch over the beds in the early spring after the ground has warmed up and before or after you have planted.

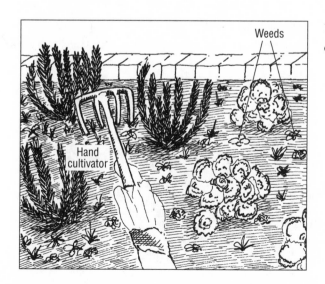

1. Cultivate the soil and pull out any existing weeds.

2. Mix together equal parts peat moss and compost. Spread mulch around plants in layers 2 to 3 inches thick. Replenish as needed. Pluck out any weeds that may appear.

Shredded and Chipped Bark and Sawdust

Shredded and chipped bark and sawdust look attractive and break down over time, adding organic matter to the soil. Chipped bark nuggets are available in various grades from fine to coarse. The large nuggets often look best around foundation plantings. Bark is expensive, but an application of large nuggets around foundation plantings will last for several years.

Sawdust is available at lumbermills and is usually free. Allow sawdust to rot for one year before applying it.

Pine Needles

Pine needles, straw, and hay can be purchased in bales at feed stores and some garden centers. Pine needles make an attractive mulch under ornamental plantings and will fade in one season to a soft, driftwood gray. They will eventually acidify the soil as they decompose. You can remedy this condition, if necessary, with applications of lime pellets, once in the spring and once in the fall.

If you plan to use fresh bark or year-old sawdust as a mulch, add 3 pounds of high-nitrogen fertilizer or cottonseed meal to the soil for each 1-inch layer of bark or sawdust that will be spread over 100 feet of ground. Mix the fertilizer into the top 2 inches of soil before spreading the mulch. This will offset the nitrogen drawn from the soil to break down the bark or sawdust into humus. When the plants are 6 inches high in the spring, mulch them following the procedure for peat moss and compost.

Straw and Hay

Straw and hay are light, porous mulches that serve as an excellent source of organic matter and nutrients as they break down. Straw and hay are not attractive in ornamental borders, but they can be used to advantage in the backs of borders or under plants whose foliage will hide the mulch. They are perfect mulches for the vegetable garden.

Follow the procedure for applying peat moss and compost. Spread straw or hay to a depth of 6 to 8 inches, tucking it around the plants.

Leaves

Leaves from fall cleanup are an ideal organic mulch for any garden and make an excellent winter mulch when mixed in equal parts with straw. Oak and beech leaves tend to be more acidic than maple leaves, but any mixture or variety is satisfactory. Rhododendrons and azaleas prefer acidity, so shredded oak leaves are superb for mulching them. Apply leaf mulches to a depth of 3 to 4 inches, following the procedure for peat moss and compost.

Grass Clippings

Grass clippings contain large amounts of nitrogen and organic matter that will benefit the soil. They make an excellent mulch—if thoroughly dried—for both flower bed and vegetable garden.

Collect grass clippings after mowing, spread them out in the sun, and allow them to dry before applying as a mulch. Fresh clippings will mat and heat up too much; put these into the compost pile. Never use grass clippings from a lawn that has been treated with an herbicide; be wary of handouts from neighbors.

Following the same procedure as for peat moss and compost, apply dried clippings to a depth of 2 to 3 inches, tucking them around plant stems.

Crushed Rock and Stone Chips

Crushed rock and stone chips are used primarily as decorative mulches. They add no nutrients to the soil, although water penetrates easily. They are best used in desert or rock gardens. They are permanent mulches and never have to be replaced.

1. First, lay black plastic, following the procedure above.
2. Using a knife, slash cross-slits every 6 inches in the plastic so that water can penetrate to the soil underneath.
3. Cover with crushed rock or stone chips to a depth that will conceal the plastic. Make additional holes in the plastic as needed to insert plants.

Directing
Plant Growth

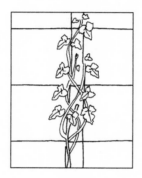

15

Staking and Tying

❧

MOST PLANTS, especially tall, blooming perennials and young trees, need support to withstand the elements. Tall, single-stemmed perennials such as delphiniums, dahlias, gladioli, and hollyhocks have a tendency to fall—ironically, at their moment of perfection—unless carefully staked. It is often necessary to support young trees to anchor the root system and to protect or straighten the trunk. Ground covers sprawl by nature, but you can direct the course of their sprawling. Timing is crucial in staking and tying plants; it must be done before the need becomes obvious.

Selecting a Stake

To choose the appropriate kind of stake, you need to know the approximate mature flowering height of the plant. Choose your stake and staking method accordingly. For example, you need much larger stakes for delphiniums, which can grow 4 or 5 feet tall, than for Michaelmas daisies, which may grow only 2 feet high.

Bamboo stakes, often painted an unobtrusive green, come in a variety of lengths and widths. A $3/4$-inch diameter is ideal for tall delphiniums, which need to have their columnar blooms secured as well as their stems. Use $1/4$-inch-diameter bamboo stakes for shorter growing annuals or perennials.

Green plastic stakes also come in various lengths and widths and function the same as bamboo stakes. Wooden stakes (usually made of redwood) vary from $1/2$ inch to 2 inches thick and are excellent for tomatoes, sunflowers, and large, showy dahlias with dinner-plate-size blooms. Plastic and wooden stakes often come with a pointed end, making them easy to insert next to the plant. If not, you can sharpen one end of a wooden stake yourself.

Branches of birch, cherry, hazel, alder, or shrubby honeysuckle are often used for support. They are sturdy and twiggy, and the plants weave through them as they mature.

Staking Tall, Single- or Multi-stemmed Perennials

Plants that need staking include delphiniums (*Delphinium* spp.), lilies (*Lilium* spp.), gladiolus (*Gladiolus* spp.), dahlias (*Dahlia* spp.), hollyhocks *(Althaea rosea),* sunflowers (*Helianthus* spp.), monkshoods (*Aconitum* species), globe thistle (*Echinops* spp.), meadow rue (*Thalictrum* spp.), fall-blooming Japanese anemones *(Anemone japonica)*, foxgloves *(Digitalis purpurea)*, coneflowers *(Echinacea purpurea)*, Canterbury bells (*Campanula* spp.), and bee balm *(Monarda didyma)*. Check a plant reference guide if you are uncertain about growing habits.

TOOLS AND SUPPLIES

3/4-inch bamboo, plastic, or wooden stakes
Soft twine
Mallet (for wooden stakes)

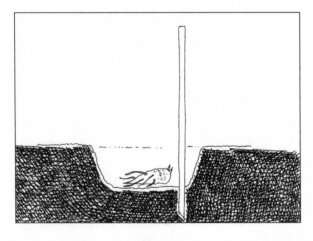

1. Stake your plant before it begins growth in the spring or when it is 6 to 8 inches high. Insert a 3/4-inch bamboo stake by hand or a wooden or plastic stake using a mallet. Drive the stake 4 to 5 inches into the ground behind the plant. For dahlia tubers, gladioli corms, or lily bulbs, drive the stake 4 to 6 inches into the ground 2 inches away from the tubers, corms, or bulbs. Try not to penetrate the plant's root system.

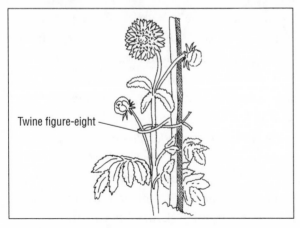

Twine figure-eight

2. As the plants grow and begin to form flower stalks, use soft twine to tie them in a loose figure eight to the stalks but in line with the support. Continue to tie up new growth as the plant matures.

Drive a single 1/2-inch bamboo stake into the center of an informal grouping of lilies or similar plants. Take care not to pierce any bulbs. Tie each stem loosely with soft twine in a figure eight or use plastic twist-ties attached to the stake.

Supporting Mounding, Bushy Plants

Mounding, bushy plants also need support. Carnations *(Dianthus)*, peonies *(Paeonia)*, chrysanthemums, Shasta daisies *(Chrysanthemum maximum)*, garden phlox *(Phlox paniculata)*, coreopsis, asters *(Aster novae-angliae* and *A. novi-belgii)*, baby's breath *(Gypsophila paniculata)*, and cranesbills *(Geranium* spp.) can be corralled and supported using one of the four following methods.

TOOLS AND SUPPLIES

Twiggy branches or bamboo or wooden stakes
Soft twine (for staked plantings)
Mallet (for wooden stakes)

1. Use a twiggy branch or branches, depending on the size of the planting. Insert the cut end of the branch or branches 4 to 6 inches into the soil behind or around the young clump. The plant will grow up and through the branches, obscuring the support system. A clump of coreopsis, for example, may require one twiggy branch; a large clump of lupines may need the support of three branches.

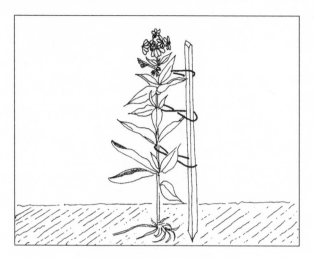

2. Drive a 1-by-1/2 inch wooden stake into the ground behind the plant, about 4 to 6 inches deep, following the procedure under Staking Tall, Single- and Multi-stemmed Perennials.

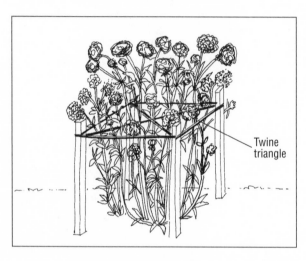

Twine triangle

3. Drive four wooden or bamboo stakes into the ground equidistant from each other, with the plant in the center. Create four triangles by crisscrossing soft twine, and tie it securely at the top of each stake.

4. For mounding plants growing in rows, use four 1-by-2-inch wooden stakes. Place a pair of them opposite each other at each end of the row, and drive them 8 inches deep into the ground. Stretch soft twine securely along each side to support the plants as they grow. Stakes should be approximately the height of the mature plants.

Anchoring Young Trees

Until a tree's root system is well established in your soil and its trunk is large enough to hold the crown erect, your new tree will need to be staked. This support is usually necessary for the first several years after transplanting to prevent damage from heavy winds. Staking a tree is a temporary measure; inspect your staked tree often to make sure the ties have not become too tight, obstructing the flow of nutrients. After your tree has been growing for a few years, remove the stakes and guy wires.

TOOLS AND SUPPLIES

Heavy guy wire (16-gauge)   Section of old plastic or rubber garden hose
Tin snips   Turnbuckles

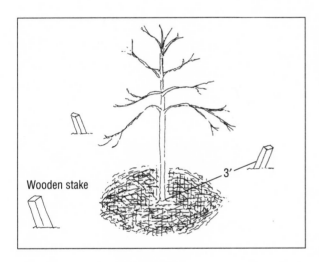

Wooden stake

1. Drive three 2-by-2-inch wooden stakes 2 feet into the ground equidistant from each other in a triangular arrangement and approximately 3 feet from the base of the tree.

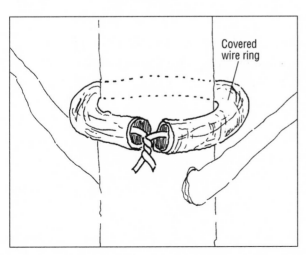

Covered wire ring

2. Using tin snips, cut a piece of wire to match the circumference of the trunk. Cover it completely with plastic or rubber hose to prevent any damage to the bark. Encircle the tree just above the second set of limbs, where the tree begins to branch out, fitting the rubber hose snugly around the trunk.

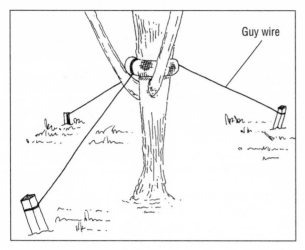

3. Attach the guy wires to the wooden stakes. Pull the guy wires from the stakes to the rubber circle, making sure each one is taut so that the tree will not bend in heavy wind.

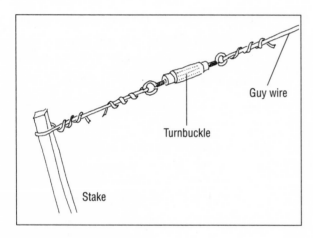

4. Use turnbuckles (see illustration) on the wires to keep them taut. Adjust each of the three guy wires by using the turn-buckles until the support is equally divided and the trunk firmly anchored. As the tree matures, adjust the length of the guy wires and the circumference of the hose-covered wire encircling the trunk, always making sure the support system is taut.

Caging Tomatoes

Tomato vines ramble by nature. To protect the fruit from insects, animals, sunscald, and disease, it should be kept off the ground. A wire mesh cylinder, placed around young plants before they flower, will help produce healthy fruit that is easy to harvest.

TOOLS AND SUPPLIES

Wooden stakes 4 feet long by 2 inches wide
5-by-7-foot sheet of concrete reinforcing
   wire with a 6-inch mesh

Heavy twine or 16-gauge aluminum wire
Mallet

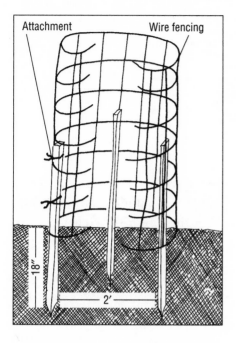

1. Using a heavy mallet, drive three 4-foot wooden stakes 18 inches into the ground and 2 feet apart, forming a triangle around the young plant. Tie one end of the concrete reinforcing wire mesh to a stake with heavy twine or wire (see illustration). Encircle the three stakes with the wire fencing until the two ends meet.

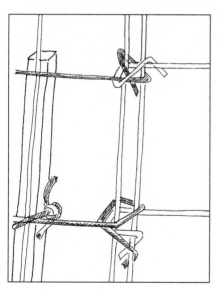

2. Secure the cylinder by bending and twisting the horizontal wires protruding from one end of the fencing around the vertical edge of the other end.

Directing Ground-cover Growth

Ground-cover plants, such as euonymus and English ivy, can be guided by a system of anchors made from coat hangers.

TOOLS AND SUPPLIES

16-gauge wire or coat hangers
Tin snips

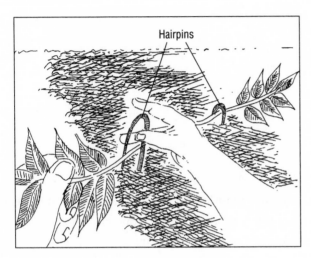

Cut 6-inch lengths of 16-gauge wire or coat hangers. Bend into hairpin shapes, and insert them over the creeping stems of ground-cover plants where you want to direct their growth.

16

Pruning

❧

GARDENERS PRUNE PLANTS to control size, direct plant growth, improve health, and increase flower and fruit production. Before pruning, look at your plants and consider how they grow naturally. Some are tall and slender with few side branches; others are bushy; still others produce arching branches. Is the allotted space in which your plants grow suitable? Often it may be necessary to make your plants conform to the dimensions of your garden.

First prune your plants to get rid of diseased or injured growth; then prune to shape. Where to cut, how to cut, and when to cut are crucial factors in pruning. Always select the right tools and the right time for the job. By understanding a few basic pruning fundamentals, you can easily direct the growth of your trees, shrubs, hedges, and vines. You will develop an artistic sense about how, where, and when to make pruning cuts. As a result, your plants will grow into attractive, productive, and manageable specimens for your garden.

TOOLS AND SUPPLIES

Gloves	Scissors-type hand pruner
Hedge shears	Loppers (long-handled pruner)
Curved pruning saw	Pruning knife
Anvil-type hand pruner	

Basic Terms

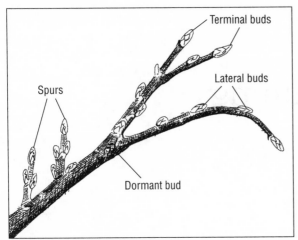

Dormant buds form on the plant during one growing season and remain dormant until the following growth period, when they develop into stems, leaves, or flowers.

Terminal buds are located at the tips of stems and produce new branches.

Lateral buds are located on the sides of branches.

Axillary buds are located at the base (or axil) of a leaf and produce flowers or leaves.

Spurs are short lateral branches with nodes located close together. They are common on fruit trees.

Nodes are the joints on a stem where leaves or buds originate.

Water sprouts are tiny, upright branches that usually grow in clumps around a large pruning wound. They are not productive and weaken the overall growth of the tree or shrub.

Suckers are branches that grow from the roots of the plant. They usually sprout from below a graft. If they are not cut off, they will grow into a wild branch or tree.

Leaders are the main trunks of a tree from which the side branches develop.

Deciduous trees and shrubs drop their leaves in the fall and winter.

Evergreen trees and shrubs keep their needles and leaves during the winter. They include the conifers (cone-bearing plants), which produce needles, and the broad-leaved evergreens, such as magnolia, holly, and camellia.

Candles are fingerlike projections on coniferous evergreens that will later produce needles.

Whorls are arrangements of three or more structures arising from a single node.

When to Prune

Late winter (when the weather is mild and the freezing is over) is a good time for pruning fruit trees, roses, broad-leaved evergreens, grapevines, and some flowering trees. Don't prune when the wood is frozen; this damages cells, and cut areas sometimes fail to heal satisfactorily.

Spring is the time for removing branches damaged by snow, wind, or ice. Do repair work now, because the sap is beginning to flow, and you can see the buds and new growth. Cut off buds that will start growth in the wrong direction, and remove suckers, water sprouts, or branches beginning to cross or grow in the wrong direction.

Early summer is a good time to shear hedges and evergreens. It is also the time to prune spring-flowering shrubs such as lilac, spirea, forsythia, and honeysuckle, after they finish flowering and before they produce new buds for the following year. Shape shrubs. Prune off limbs or branches that may form bad crotches or suckers on young trees.

Late summer, when growth has stopped but before the leaves fall, is a good time to prune maple and birch trees, which bleed too much in the winter or spring. This is also the best time to prune the basal portions of evergreens, if necessary.

Fall is the ideal time for pruning roses, clematis, hydrangea, buddleia, crape myrtle, and potentilla. Woody vines, such as wisteria, trumpet vine, and climbing hydrangea, can be pruned in fall as well.

Where and What to Prune

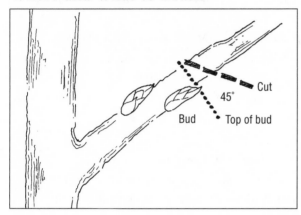

• Cut off dead, diseased, or broken branches anytime you notice them. After cutting off a diseased branch, wipe your lopper or pruner blades with alcohol to prevent the spread of infection.

• Make all cuts back to a bud, branch, main trunk, or ground level. Follow the old maxim "Never leave a stub you can hang your hat on." Large stubs encourage disease and decay. A cut should never be too close to or too far from the bud.

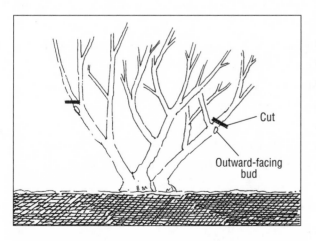

• Cut from an outward-facing bud so that the stem will grow toward an open space, not into another branch, causing congestion.

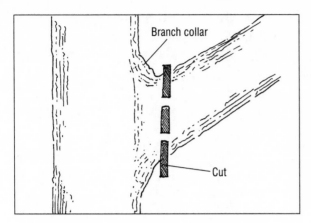

• Do not paint pruning cuts or wounds. If a branch is cut off from the trunk, just along the outer edge of the branch collar, the tree produces its own wound-healing chemicals.

• Young trees should always be pruned early. If a tree normally has one trunk, or leader, make certain that only one trunk develops.

• Cut suckers from the base of grafted trees or shrubs. Many ornamental plants, such as roses, lilacs, and crab apples, are grafted or budded. This graft or bud is usually only a foot or less below ground level. If suckers are allowed to develop, they will spoil the symmetry of the plant and sap strength from the variety you want.

Popular Ornamental Trees

Bayberry *(Myrica pensylvanica)*. Prune to remove suckers or winter injury.

Cherry, peach, plum, flowering almond *(Prunus spp.)*. Prune to shape in late winter.

Cranberry bush, nannyberry, blackhaw, and cultivars *(Viburnum spp.)*. Prune in late winter only when branches become congested.

European hornbeam *(Carpinus betulus)*. Prune to tree form.

Flowering dogwood and Kousa dogwood *(Cornus florida* and *C. kousa)*. Prune as little as possible; these trees are slow to heal.

Golden-shower, or senna *(Cassia fistula)*. Cut back the season's growth to short spurs after blooming.

Hawthorn *(Crataegus spp.)*. Prune to shape in late winter.

Oriental hornbeam *(Carpinus orientalis)*. Prune to tree form.

Redbud *(Cercis canadensis)*. Prune after blooming if needed.

Russian olive *(Elaeagnus pungens)*. Prune only to control size, if necessary, in late winter.

Shadbush, or serviceberry *(Amelanchier spp.)*. Prune to shape or to remove broken branches only.

Smoketree *(Cotinus obovatus)*. Prune to grow as bush or small tree. Cut off fading flowers.

Pruning Deciduous Trees

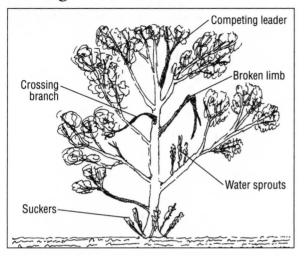

Before you begin to prune a deciduous tree, consider its natural appearance. Always try to preserve its characteristic look. Use a curved pruning saw or loppers to remove dead or broken limbs and crossed branches. Snip off any water sprouts arising at the branches or suckers coming up at the base of the trunk.

If your tree is less than two years old remove side branches with weak crotches or V-shaped angles. Also remove branches that are too close to the ground. The tree should have a strong main trunk, or leader, so remove completely any competing trunk stem.

Three Basic Shapes for Fruit Trees

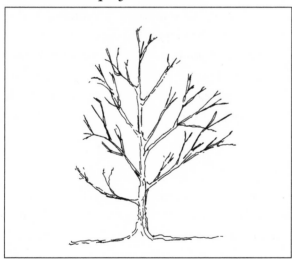

1. The *central leader shape* emphasizes one tall main trunk, or leader, with branches growing in tiers from it. This shape allows sunlight to reach into the branches, encouraging more fruit production and discouraging scab, mildew, and other diseases. Eventually, it may be necessary to remove the top of the central leader if it becomes top-heavy and sags under heavy loads of fruit. The procedure will not harm the tree and will also prevent it from growing too tall. This shape is excellent for apple and pear trees.

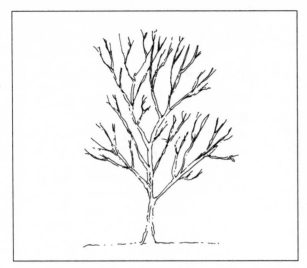

2. The *modified leader shape* is comparable to the central leader shape, but here you encourage the central leader to branch off to form several tops. This method ensures that the loads of fruit at the top of the tree are never as heavy as those at the bottom, where the limbs tend to be larger. Cut back the top occasionally to shorten the tree or to allow more sunlight to reach inside the branches. The modified leader shape is easy to maintain because most apple and pear trees grow this way naturally.

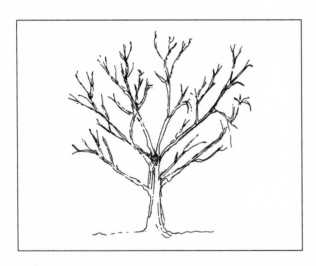

3. The *open-center method* (open top or vase shape) is ideal for smaller fruit trees such as quince, crab apple, and plum. Prune so that the limbs forming the vase shape do not all come from the main trunk. This method produces a short trunk and an open center with three or four main branches. The whole center of the tree remains open, and the maturing fruit receives adequate sunlight and air circulation.

Pruning Fruit Trees at Planting Time

Fruit trees should be pruned after they are planted. When you prune a fruit tree, make your cuts to the lateral outside bud so that the tree will sprout outward as it grows. Always keep in mind the natural growth habit of the mature tree. Keep branches sparse so that sunlight will reach the developing fruit.

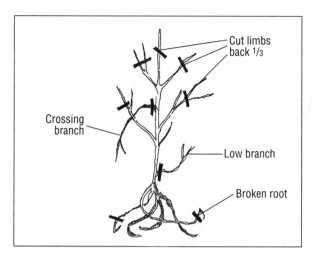

1. Cut off any jagged or broken roots. If the tree has branches, cut all the limbs back by one-third. Cut off any broken branches and any branches closer than 18 to 24 inches from the ground.

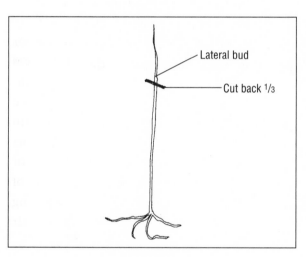

2. Cut back trees that are whips (have no branches) by one-third. For example, if a whip is 6 feet tall, cut 2 feet off the top. Make the cut just below the lateral bud.

Pruning Conifers

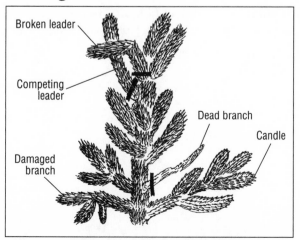

When pruning a coniferous tree, consider its natural shape as a guide. Cut out diseased wood or broken limbs whenever you see them. If a leader is broken, prune it and choose another to dominate. At the same time, remove any competing leaders. Consider carefully before you cut off any sweeping branches (large lower branches that might touch the ground), because once removed, they will not regrow.

Pines should be pruned in early summer before the candles harden. Spruces, which are more tolerant, can be trimmed into the summer. Remove no more than one-third of the new wood each year. Juniper and cypress can be pruned safely at any time, although early spring to late July is best. Wear gloves when pruning conifers, because abrasions from needles may cause skin rashes.

Determinate Conifers

Determinate conifers are those whose branches radiate from the trunk in whorls. These include fir (*Abies* spp.), spruce (*Picea* spp.), and pine (*Pinus* spp.). Do not cut back to old wood. These conifers do not have latent buds on the older wood behind the foliage. Do not prune the leader, or you will destroy the natural appearance of the tree.

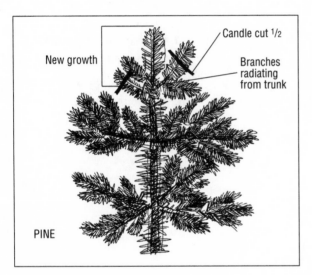

To prune a pine, cut off half of the candle as it is expanding. The branch will grow half the size. To prune other determinate conifers, cut off the new growth to a bud.

Indeterminate Conifers

Indeterminate conifers produce branches that radiate in a random fashion. They contain many buds all along the branches. These include arborvitae (*Thuja* and *Platycladus* spp.), hemlock (*Tsuga* spp.), juniper (*Juniperus* spp.), and yew (*Taxus* spp.).

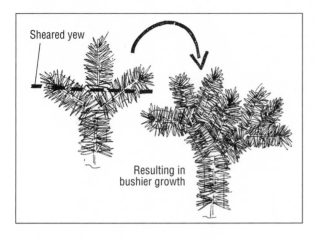

Sheared yew

Resulting in bushier growth

To prune an indeterminate conifer, cut back to old wood or shear lightly as a hedge.

Pruning Deciduous Shrubs

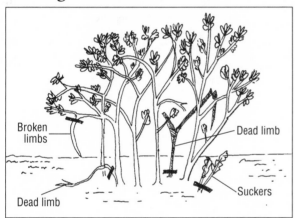

Broken limbs

Dead limb

Dead limb

Suckers

When pruning a shrub, try to preserve the natural shape of the species. Remove any diseased, dead, or damaged branches. Prune out any crossing branches. Cut back to a bud or branch that points in the direction you want the new growth to pursue. Thin all dense growth so that sunlight will reach the inner branches; this will promote larger blooms and healthier foliage. Prune all spring-flowering shrubs immediately after they finish blooming.

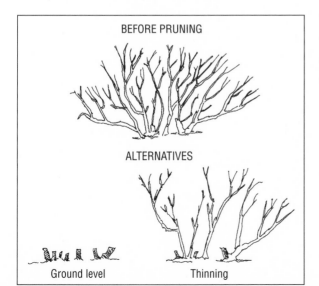

BEFORE PRUNING

ALTERNATIVES

Ground level   Thinning

To rejuvenate old shrubs that have grown too tall and ungainly, such as mock orange, forsythia, lilac, or spirea, you have two choices.

1. Cut off the entire shrub to 6 inches above the ground in the early spring, and allow it to regrow as a new plant.

2. Alternatively, thin out the old growth by cutting off older branches near the ground and allowing new ones to form.

Shearing Hedges

Shearing removes the terminal buds on all stem tips, and a new flush of growth appears behind the cuts. Hedges of yew and boxwood take well to shearing. Always use sharp hedge shears with long blades and long handles. The best time to cut a hedge is when it's growing fast—usually in late spring. For those that grow over longer periods, such as holly, privet, and barberry, you may have to trim several times a season. Trim hedges when you think they need to be trimmed; never wait until they are too tall and floppy.

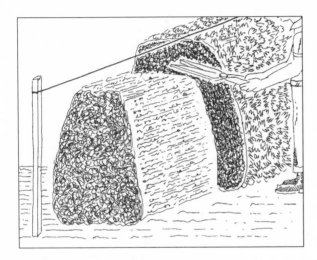

Don't ignore the sides of a hedge. Shear the plants so that the bottom is wider than the top. All side branches will then receive adequate sunlight, and the top will not become top-heavy, breaking under heavy snow and ice.

Easy-maintenance Evergreen Hedges
American arborvitae *(Thuja occidentalis)*
Canada hemlock *(Tsuga canadensis)*
Holly (*Ilex* spp.)
Spruce (*Picea* spp.)
Yew *(Taxus x media 'Hicksii')*

Easy-maintenance Deciduous Hedges
Barberry (*Berberis* spp.)
Boxwood (*Buxus sempervirens* and *B. microphylla* var. *koreana*)
Burning bush (*Euonymus alatus* 'Compactus')
Forsythia (*Forsythia* spp.)
Privet (*Ligustrum* spp.)

Pruning Woody, Ornamental, and Flowering Vines

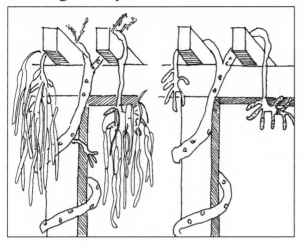

Each year, in the late dormant season, cut vines back and pull out any weak or dead branches to a healthy branch. Prune a vine back to a lateral branch or bud, and do not leave a stub. If the vine has become unmanageable from lack of pruning, cut it to the ground and allow it to start over. If the vine flowers on old wood, do not remove this wood (unless it is necessary to thin the vine), or you will sacrifice flowers. This is true of some climbing roses, clematis, and honeysuckle. If uncertain, check with a reliable nursery.

Flowering climbers fall into two groups: the early flowering (prune immediately after flowering) and the late flowering (prune the following spring).

Early-flowering Climbers

Clematis (*Clematis montana, C. macropetala,* and *C. 'Belle of Woking'*)

Fiveleaf akebia *(Akebia quinata)*

Honeysuckle (*Lonicera* spp.)

Summer jasmine *(Jasminum officinale)*

Wisteria (*Wisteria* spp.) (may require several prunings a season)

Late-flowering Climbers

Clematis (*Clematis* x *jackmanii, C.* 'Ville de Lyon', and *C.* 'Nelly Moser')

Trumpet vine *(Campsus radicans)*

Winter jasmine *(Jasminum nudiflorum)*

17

Deadheading, Pinching, and Disbudding

ॐ

To DIRECT PLANT GROWTH during the season, it is necessary to deadhead, pinch, and disbud your annuals, perennials, and some flowering shrubs. Deadheading often produces a second flush of blooms. Pinching encourages branching, and each branch tip produces a flower truss. The more attention you pay to those tasks, the more flowers your plants will produce. Disbudding, on the other hand, is a form of thinning so that the plant will concentrate its strength into producing a single, magnificent bloom on each stem. Deadheading also prevents invasive plants, such as Johnnie jump-ups, poppies, chives, and portulaca, from self-sowing all over the garden, and it keeps your beds looking neater.

These techniques are easy and can be done in a matter of minutes, or even seconds. As a result, your perennials, annuals, and shrubs will perform at their peak throughout the season.

TOOLS AND SUPPLIES
Pruning shears
Scissors
Hedge shears

Deadheading
Deadheading Perennials
For perennials that bloom only once a season, such as peonies, bearded iris, and daylilies, remove the faded flowers and stems to strengthen the plant. For other perennials, such as hosta, ligularia, marsh marigold, and delphinium, cut the stems with pruning shears at the base of the plant after the flowers have faded to promote more blooms the same season.

With the stem between thumb and forefinger, pinch off just above the set of leaves nearest the faded bloom. If the stems are thick, use pruning shears.

Deadheading Annuals

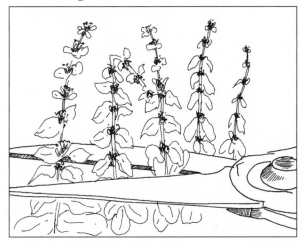

After blooms have faded on petunias and soft-stemmed multiflowering plants, such as arabis, alyssum, ajuga, nierembergia, and yarrow, trim them back. If you have masses of these bedding plants in your garden, it is easiest to make a clean cut halfway down the stems using a pair of hedge shears. For taller annuals, marigolds, dahlias, zinnias, salvias, wallflowers, and larkspurs, deadhead using your fingernails or pruning shears to prevent your plants from becoming leggy.

The annual wax begonia (Begonia semperflorens) requires no deadheading. It never sets seed and is perfect for sun or partial shade.

Deadheading Shrubs

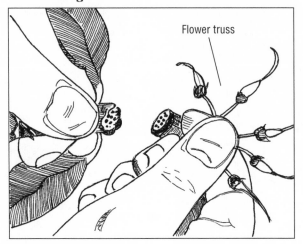

Flower truss

Rhododendrons, azaleas, mountain laurel, Japanese pieris or andromeda, and lilacs need careful deadheading. Remove flower clusters just as they fade and before they set seed. Gently bend them to one side, then snap them off between your thumb and forefinger. If the shrub is large and simply covered with blooms, don't waste your time removing all the spent flowers; let common sense be your guide.

Pinching
Pinching Perennials

To increase the size of flowers on perennials that produce a thicket of stems, pinch young shoots off near ground level in spring when they are 4 to 6 inches tall. Leave four or five shoots in each clump. Because there are fewer stalks for the plant to feed, the clump will grow vigorously and produce larger blooms. This method is particularly effective with phlox and Michaelmas daisies.

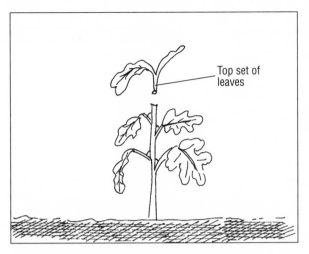

Fall-blooming perennials, such as chrysanthemums, hardy asters, boltonias, and sneezeweed, need pinching. Begin when plants are 6 inches tall by pinching the tip of each stem, including the top set of leaves. Repeat pinching each time new shoots grow out 6 inches. Stop pinching in midsummer to allow flower buds to develop. This results in shorter stems and smaller flowers, but the flowers are more numerous.

Pinching Annuals

For single-stemmed annuals, such as Shasta daisies, dahlias, zinnias, large-flowered marigolds, stock, wallflowers, and snapdragons, pinch off the growing stem tips in spring when plants are 6 inches tall to encourage branching. A bushier plant produces more flowers. (See illustration.)

Disbudding

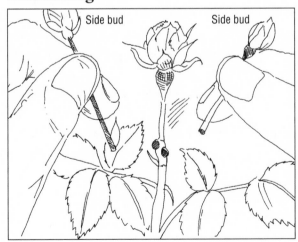

Disbudding is a special kind of thinning. Instead of eliminating entire stems, you remove a few side buds from a stem to produce a larger, showy bloom. For example, if a rose stem contains four buds, removing three of these buds along the side will produce a single, larger rose. Removing side flower buds on delphinium and foxglove will produce bigger, single flowerstalks. Disbudding often results in heavy blooms that require staking, however.

18

Training Vines

🙠

Vines are attractive additions to any planting scheme. They offer quick and easy solutions for creating shade and camouflage, as well as softening effects on fences and walls. In addition to their decorative foliage, some vines produce showy and fragrant blooms, such as the honeysuckles, morning glories, and climbing hydrangea. As in choosing any plant for your garden, the right plant for the right place is of vital importance in selecting vines. Some vines may even be used as ground covers. Where they have room to sprawl and develop, they can rapidly cover banks and slopes.

To use vines effectively, you need to have some knowledge of the plant's habits. For example, a vine that clings, such as Boston ivy, will not do well on a wall trellis, and a clematis with tendrils that grab can't attach itself to thick crosspieces such as those of a wooden trellis.

Common Garden Vines
Twining vines have stems that wind around a trellis. They include the following common garden vines:

Bittersweet (*Celastrus* spp.). Deciduous perennial.

Carolina jessamine *(Gelsemium sempervirens)*. Evergreen perennial.

Japanese honeysuckle *(Lonicera japonica)*. Evergreen perennial.

Moonflower *(Ipomoea alba)*. Perennial grown as annual.

Morning glory *(Ipomoea imperialis)*. Annual.

Nasturtium (climbing type) *(Tropaeolum majus)*. Annual.

Star jasmine *(Trachelospermum jasminoides)*. Evergreen perennial.

Wisteria (*Wisteria* spp.). Deciduous perennial.

Vines with tendrils that grab and wrap around a trellis or wire support include the following common varieties:

Grape (*Vitis* spp.). Deciduous perennial.

Passion flower (*Passiflora* spp.). Evergreen perennial.

Sweet pea *(Lathyrus odoratus)*. Annual.

Trumpet vine *(Campsus radicans)*. Deciduous perennial.

Other vines produce holdfasts, disclike tips or aerial roots that adhere to a brick, stone, or concrete surface. They include the following common varieties:

Boston ivy *(Parthenocissus tricuspidata)*. Deciduous perennial.

Climbing hydrangea (*Hydrangea anomala* subsp. *petiolaris*). Deciduous perennial.

Climbing fig *(Ficus pumila)*. Evergreen perennial.

English ivy *(Hedera helix)*. Evergreen perennial.

Trumpet vine *(Campsis radicans)*. Deciduous perennial.

Virginia creeper *(Parthenocissus quinquefolia)*. Deciduous perennial.

Training Vines to Grow on Walls or Wooden Fencing

Vines growing on walls and fences enhance the visual lushness of the garden. Trumpet vine *(Campsis radicans)*, Dutchman's-pipe *(Aristolochia durior)*, and porcelain berry *(Ampelopsis brevipedunculata)* are often used for this purpose.

TOOLS AND SUPPLIES

Ruler   Lag eyes

Pencil   Light-gauge wire, fishing line, or twine

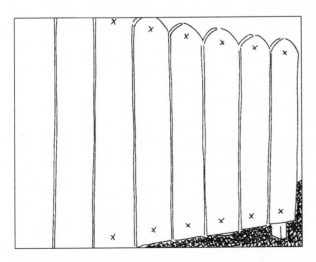

1. Using a ruler and pencil, mark off points 4 to 6 inches apart and equidistant from each other along a straight line at the top of the area where you intend to train your vine. Repeat the above process at the bottom of the area.

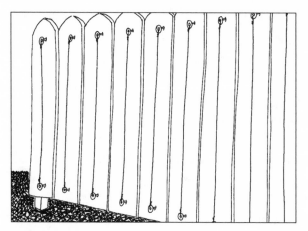

2. Insert lag eyes at each point, top and bottom, so that they will secure the wire or twine 1 inch from the fence or wall. Stretch light-gauge wire, fishing line, or twine from each lag eye at the top to the corresponding lag eye at the bottom. Make sure each line is taut and secure.

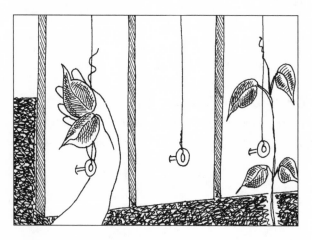

3. Train vines when growth begins by guiding each one manually to a vertical support. They will take off on their own within a week.

Alternative Designs

You can vary the above design by using one of the following alternatives.

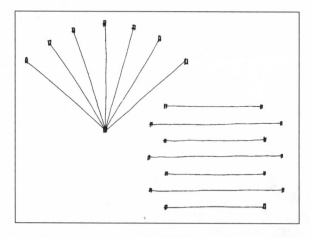

1. Create a fan-shaped pattern by inserting only one lag eye at the bottom of a fence section or wall and a series of lag eyes, equidistant from each other, at the top. Stretch light-gauge wire, fishing line, or twine from the lag eye at the bottom to each of those at the top.

2. Insert lag eyes on each side, and stretch supports horizontally.

Training Vines to Grow on Hard Surfaces

You may want to grow vines on the house or on another hard-surface structure. Try using English ivy *(Hedera helix 'Baltica'),* Climbing hydrangea *(Hydrangea anomala* subsp. *petiolaris),* or Boston ivy *(Parthenocissus tricuspidata).*

TOOLS AND SUPPLIES

Concrete nails or adhesive discs with hooks
(available at hardware stores and garden centers)

Super Glue
Light-gauge wire, fishing line, or twine

1. On brick, stone, or stucco walls, drive concrete nails or attach adhesive discs with Super Glue. Space them 4 to 6 inches apart and equidistant from each other.

2. Stretch light-gauge wire, fishing line, or twine between the nails or discs, making sure each line is taut.

Training Vines to Grow on a Net Fence

A net fence is ideal for cucumbers, peas, and pole beans. Erect the fence as soon as you have planted your seeds or when the plants are no more than 3 inches tall.

TOOLS AND SUPPLIES

Two angle-iron fence stakes, 6 to 8 feet long with
pierced support holes
Plastic netting with 4-inch-square mesh

Twist-ties or soft twine
Shears

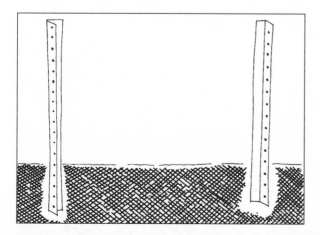

1. Drive a stake 2 feet deep at each end of the row.

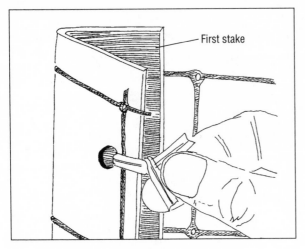

First stake

2. Attach a piece of netting 1 foot longer than the row of plants to the stake at one end by inserting plastic twist-ties or soft twine through the top hole in the stake and around the edge of the net. Continue in this manner down the stake.

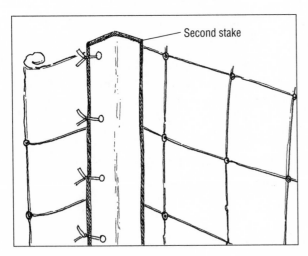

Second stake

3. After the net is secured to the first stake, pull it across to the second. Make sure it is taut, then repeat the tying procedure.

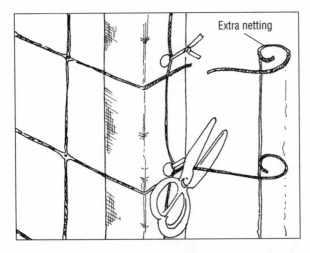

Extra netting

4. Trim off any extra netting along the side of the second stake, and cut the bottom of the net 3 inches from ground level.

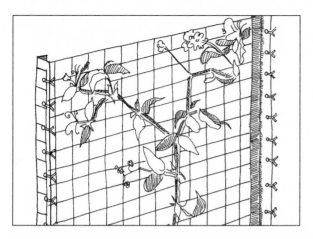

5. Train young plants as they climb by pushing tendrils into the mesh. Take care not to snap tender stems.

Growing Vines on a Lamppost

Climbing roses, clematis, morning glories, and sweetpeas are commonly used for growing on lampposts.

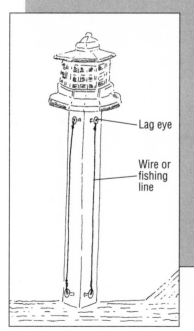

Lag eye

Wire or
fishing
line

To train vines onto a wooden lamppost, insert a lag eye at the top and bottom of each of the four sides of the post. Stretch light-gauge wire, fishing line, or twine tautly between each pair of lag eyes. Guide the young vine by hand for several weeks until it is established.

To train vines onto a metal lamppost, tie each maturing stem or rose cane to the post with soft twine or plastic twist-ties. Do not use wire, which may cut into the stems or canes as they mature.

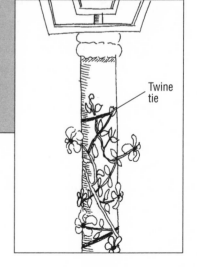

Twine
tie

19

Growing Grapes

୫ର

THE GRAPE IS ONE OF THE OLDEST FRUITS in cultivation. It is grown for jelly, wine, juice, and shade. To establish a productive grapevine on your property, you need ordinary soil, good drainage, full sun, and the patience to follow an annual three-year pruning cycle. This pruning takes very little physical labor and occurs only once a year, and it is essential for a healthy grapevine. If you want to grow grapevines simply for shade, you need to prune annually in the spring to prevent them from becoming overgrown and congested. But if you want to harvest fruit, you must annually prune off old wood over one year old.

All grape varieties are self-pollinating, and you don't need to plant different strains in order to harvest fruit. If you live in a cold region of the country (zone 4, 5, or 6) try Interlaken Seedless, Concord, or Steuben. For the best varieties to plant in your area, consult your local county extension service.

The directions that follow are for planting and maintaining one grapevine. If you wish to grow several varieties, you can build an arbor with parallel posts and overhead supports.

TOOLS AND SUPPLIES

Three pressure-treated 2-by-4s or 3- to
   4-inch-diameter cedar posts 6 feet long
Shovel or posthole digger
One 36-foot roll of smooth 9- to
   10-gauge wire

Three bags of ready-mix concrete (optional)
Nine lag eyes
Narrow plastic ribbon
Hand pruners

Erecting the Post-and-wire Support

Select the location carefully. It should have good drainage, and your vine must receive sun all day.

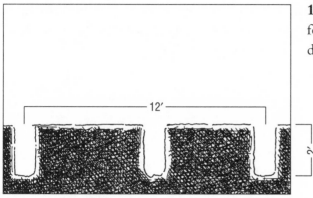

1. Dig two postholes 2 feet deep and 12 feet apart. Dig a third posthole 2 feet deep midway between the two.

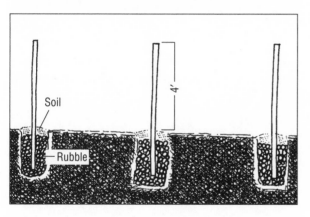

2. Place each post in a hole. Make sure they are perpendicular to the ground and parallel with one another. Each should stand 4 feet above ground level. Backfill each hole with rubble and soil, and tamp down firmly. Alternatively, fill around them with ready-mix concrete, and allow to dry for twenty-four hours before further work.

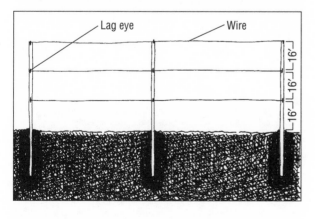

3. Insert three lag eyes on each post: the first, 16 inches from ground level; the next, 16 inches from the first (in the middle); and the last, at the top. Stretch wire from post to post through the corresponding lag eyes and pull taut. Secure the wires by twisting the ends around each lag eye.

Preparing the Soil and Planting the Grapevine

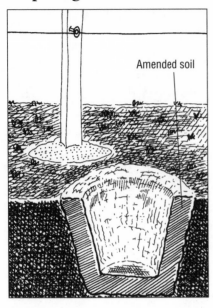

Amended soil

1. Dig a hole for the grapevine 1 foot away from the center post so that you will not loosen it. Make the hole 1 foot deep and 1 foot wide. Amend the soil with compost and organic matter. If you are planting more than one vine, the planting distance between vines should be a minimum of 8 feet.

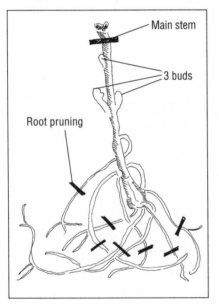

Main stem

3 buds

Root pruning

2. Cut the roots of the vine back to 6 inches. Cut the stem to three buds. Plant the vine and water it thoroughly.

Pruning and Training the Grapevine

Initial training and annual spring pruning are critical for growing a productive grapevine. Pruning will encourage the growth of a sturdy main stem, or trunk, that will produce lateral, fruiting canes. The purpose of pruning is to limit fruit production and to control cane growth so that the cane and fruit are in balance at all times. If planted and pruned carefully, a single vine can develop into one of your garden's most outstanding features.

The First Year

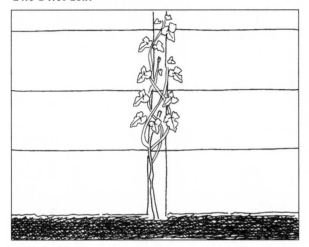

1. During the summer of the first full growing season, three shoots will grow up. In the early winter, after growth has stopped, tie each of these shoots to the central post with narrow plastic ribbon. Do not use tape or wire, which might damage the tender bark.

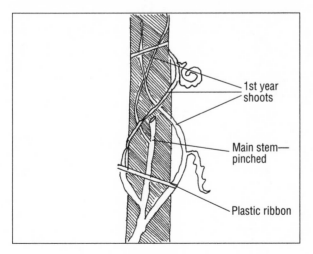

1st year shoots

Main stem—pinched

Plastic ribbon

2. Pinch the growing point of the main stem.

The Second Year

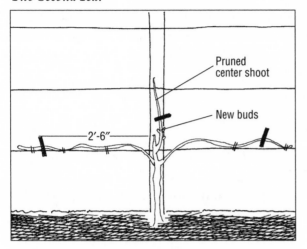

Pruned center shoot

New buds

2'-6"

1. In the spring of the vine's second year, tie the two strongest shoots to the bottom wire, one on each side of the trunk. Prune the center shoot back to leave only three buds. Prune each side shoot back to 2¹/2 feet from the trunk. During the second summer, the central shoot will produce three shoots. Tie these to the central post.

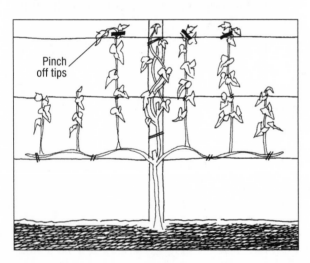

Pinch off tips

2. Over the second summer, the horizontal shoots will produce side shoots. Tie the side shoots to the wire above. As they grow longer, tie them again to the top wire and pinch off their tips.

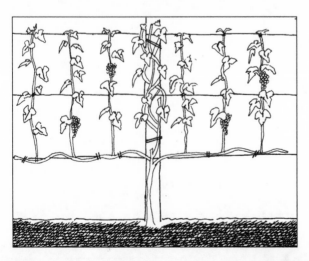

3. In the first fruiting year, allow only four bunches of grapes to mature.

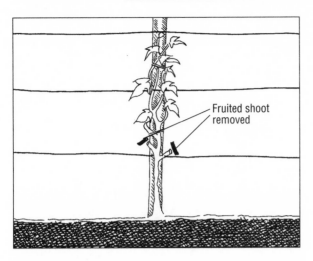

Fruited shoot removed

4. After picking, cut out the fruited shoots.

The Third Year

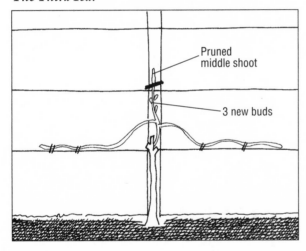

Pruned middle shoot

3 new buds

1. In late winter, tie two shoots from the central post to the side wires.

2. Cut back the middle shoot. Each year, the side shoots can be allowed to grow longer, producing more fruit, until you have covered your post-and-wire framework.

Every three years, begin the process over again, as described for the first year, to maintain your vine.

Lawn Care and Maintenance

20

Planting a Lawn

☙

A SUCCESSFUL, HEALTHY LAWN should be comfortable to walk on, spongy and cool to bare feet on a hot summer's day, a safe place for children to play, a green carpet that is really an extension of your living area. The soft, eye-pleasing color of a healthy lawn highlights everything else in the garden.

To make a good lawn the right way is not easy, but if you follow each step in the process—choosing the best seed, tilling and grading the area, digging in organic matter and other amendments—you can't go wrong.

Selecting the Right Grass Seed

You can buy grass seed in pure varieties or as a blend. An experienced garden store owner can advise you on the best variety and the amount of seed you will need for your zone. Consider the amount of sunlight in the new lawn area before you select your seed.

Cool-season Grasses

Cool-season grasses withstand winter cold but do not thrive where the summers are long and hot. They are best planted in northern areas in spring or fall.

Bents require a lot of maintenance. They need careful fertilizing, watering, and mowing, and they grow best in full sun. They should not be allowed to grow higher than 1 inch. They are often planted in cool, wet areas of the country, such as the Pacific Northwest. Use them for a showplace lawn that receives little foot traffic.

Fine fescues are included in most fine-leaved lawn mixtures. The leaves look like tiny, soft needles. Fescues are easily grown in most soils. They are fairly drought resistant and shade tolerant.

Bluegrasses are widely grown and available in most mixtures. Only one variety, *Poa trivalis,* does well in shade.

Rye grasses come in perennial and annual varieties. They are rapid growers but have a bunchy growth habit and are often hard to mow.

Coarse fescues are rugged and are good for athletic fields and children's play yards. They do best in full sun.

Clover is popular in some low-maintenance grass mixtures. It is a rapid grower and manufactures its own nitrogen, thereby reducing the need for much fertilizing. Beware of planting clover, however, if a member of your household is allergic to bee stings.

Redtop is often included in grass mixtures. It serves as a temporary nurse crop until other grasses take hold.

Wheatgrass is a cold-weather, drought-resistant, bunching turf grass that requires full sun. It grows well in any garden soil and is excellent for a lawn where foot traffic is high. Mow to a height of 2 inches.

Subtropical Grasses

Subtropical grasses are warm-season grasses that grow actively during the summer months, then become dormant. They are best planted in late spring or early summer.

Zoysia grass is very slow to establish but eventually forms a strong, dense turf resistant to weeds, insects, and diseases. It goes dormant in winter, and the lawn area will remain brown for many months. It is quite drought resistant and easy to maintain in sun or shade.

Bahia grass is a coarse-textured grass that does well in hot, dry climates and poor, sandy soil. Mow it to a height of 2 to 3 inches.

Bermuda grass is fine textured, and new hybrid strains of are very popular, but this grass will not flourish in shade.

Buffalograss is a warm-season, transitional turf grass requiring full sun and alkaline soil. This fine-textured, low-growing grass forms a tight sod. Mow to a height of 1/2 to 1 1/4 inches.

St. Augustine grass is a coarse, dark green, wide-bladed grass that is extremely easy to maintain. It has a short dormancy period and will tolerate some shade. This grass needs frequent mowing.

Planting Grass Seed

Seeding is the most common and least expensive method for covering a major area or simply a bare patch that needs attention.

TOOLS AND SUPPLIES

Rotary tiller (for large areas)   Old tire, attached to a rope for pulling
Shovel   Hand-held or drop spreader
Garden rake   Commercial lawn fertilizer (10–5–5 or 12–4–8)
Metal lawn roller   Fine-mist nozzle for watering
Wheelbarrow

1. Till the area using a rotary tiller, or if you are sowing a bare patch or a small area, dig with a shovel to a 6-inch depth, chopping up the clods as you progress.

2. Remove all stones, roots, and other debris, then rake the area smooth.

3. Now pull an old tire, attached to a rope and lying flat on its side, back and forth to cover the area. Then, pull the tire in the same manner in a direction perpendicular to the first. This procedure will level out any small hills and hollows. Pull the tire over the area four or five times to smooth the freshly dug soil and help improve drainage. An alternative to this process is simply to use a garden rake to level the area as much as possible.

4. Water the area thoroughly once a day for one week. The freshly tilled soil will settle, and weed seeds will sprout. Wait about three weeks, allowing the weed seeds to sprout but not allowing the weeds to go to seed, then repeat the tilling, raking, and grading procedure. The clumps of weeds will be tilled under.

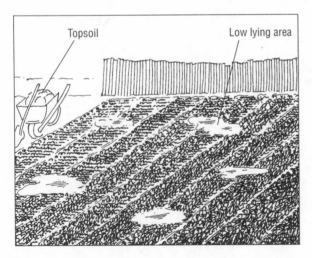

5. After the second tilling, add topsoil to low-lying areas that need to be raised for better drainage.

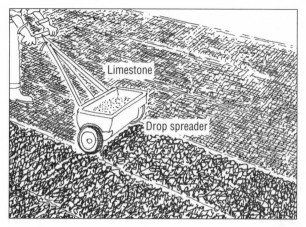

6. If the pH level of your soil is below 6, add powdered limestone to lower the soil acidity. Use 50 to 80 pounds of lime per 1,000 square feet of lawn. Sprinkle it evenly over the area by hand or use a drop spreader. Each trail of lime should exactly meet the trail beside it without overlapping. If your soil is quite acid, repeat this procedure every three to four years in the spring.

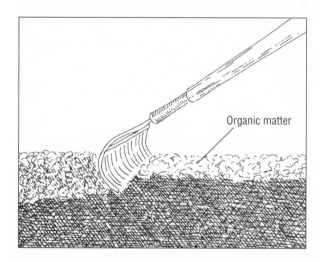

7. Scatter shovelfuls of organic matter, such as rotted sawdust or peat moss, over the soil surface. Rake it thoroughly into the tilled surface to a depth of 1 or 2 inches.

8. Roll the bed once with a light metal lawn roller filled with only a couple inches of water.

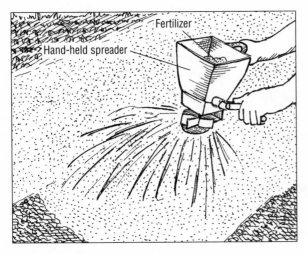

9. Spread a commercial fertilizer evenly over the area using a hand–held or drop spreader. Follow the directions on the bag. Do not overfertilize.

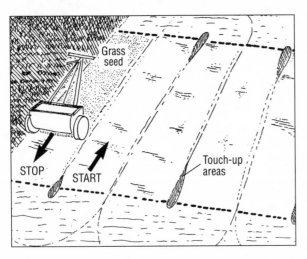

10. Sow grass seed using a hand–held or drop spreader; 1/2 ounce (two handfuls) per square yard is generally recommended. If you use a drop spreader, touch up by hand the corners or edges missed by the spreader.

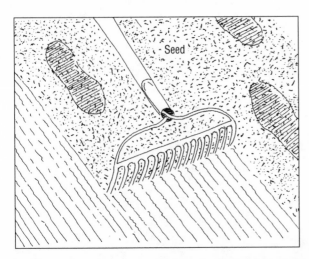

11. After you spread fertilizer and seed, smooth out the area with a garden rake. Do this gently, just one time, in a row–by–row pattern. Walk backward, dragging the rake in front of you, to avoid leaving footprints. The new grass should germinate in a fine, even pattern.

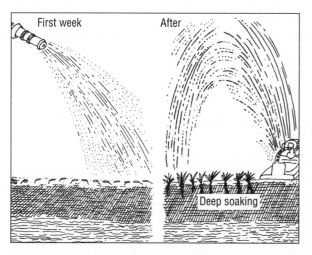

First week

After

Deep soaking

12. For the first week, gently water by hand for a half hour twice a day with a fine-mist nozzle attached to a garden hose. The seed should germinate within seven days. After most of the seed has germinated, use a sprinkler. Keep track of the time, and move the sprinkler around for even coverage. A long soaking is preferable to several short ones, as it will encourage grass roots to grow more deeply.

Check your new lawn daily. Never let it dry out. A healthy, green lawn requires 1 inch of water per week. Don't walk or play on the area for at least six weeks. Six weeks after sowing, when the grass is 2 to 3 inches high, mow the lawn to a height of 1 1/2 inches. Your mower should have sharp blades. This will prevent grass from going to seed and browning out.

Fertilize your lawn with a commercial lawn fertilizer twice a year, spring and fall. Follow the directions on the bag. Avoid any fertilizer that contains an herbicide or weed killer.

To help your grass survive during dry seasons or when water is restricted, cut grass less often and raise the cutting height, don't fertilize, and where possible, eliminate weeds that compete with grass for moisture.

21

Laying Sod

❧

THE QUICKEST WAY TO ESTABLISH A LAWN is to lay commercially grown sod. This sod is harvested in strips 6 to 9 feet long, 2 feet wide, and 3/4 to 1 inch thick, and is sold in rolls for easy installation. It is more costly than a seeded lawn, but you can enjoy green grass instantly. Sod is ideal for steep slopes because the roots knit quickly, if properly installed and watered, and erosion is halted.

TOOLS AND SUPPLIES

Rotary tiller (for large areas)   Spade or sharp knife with serrated edge
Shovel   Metal lawn roller
Garden rake   Fine-mist nozzle for watering
Wheelbarrow

Laying Sod on a Flat Area

Complete your soil preparation work in advance of the delivery date for your pieces of sod, called *turves*. Turves should be laid as soon as they arrive. If you must wait several days before laying sod, keep it moistened; dried sod will not revive.

6″

1. Till the area using a rotary tiller or, if you are laying sod in a small area, dig with a shovel to a 6-inch depth, chopping up the clods as you progress.

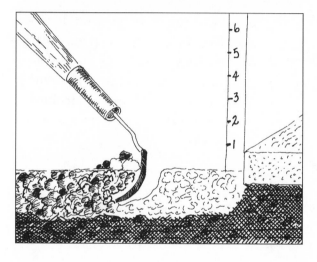

6
5
4
3
2
1

2. Remove all stones, roots, and other debris. Rake the area smooth. The final grade should be ³/4 inch lower than sidewalks or driveways to allow for the thickness of the sod.

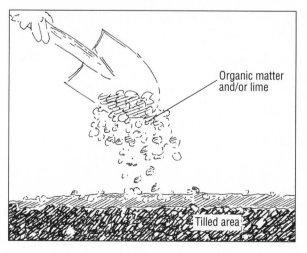

Organic matter and/or lime

Tilled area

3. Apply organic matter, such as rotted sawdust or peat moss, and lime if the soil's pH level is below 6. Scatter shovelfuls over the area, then rake it thoroughly into the tilled surface to a depth of 1 or 2 inches. Do not apply commercial fertilizer at this time. If you install your sod in the spring, fertilize it in the fall; if installing in the fall, fertilize the next spring.

Turves

4. If the area you have prepared for your sod is dry, sprinkle it with water *before* you lay your turves. The soil should be damp but not muddy. Begin by unrolling the first strip of sod along a straight edge such as a driveway or walk. Handle the sod strips carefully; do not stretch or pull them.

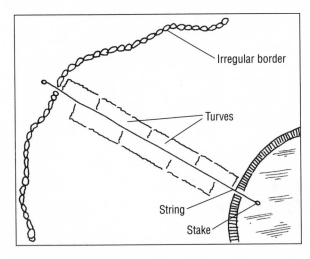

Irregular border

Turves

String

Stake

5. If the area is irregular on all sides, stretch a string across the middle of the area, pull taut, and secure to stakes at each end. Begin by unrolling the first turves on either side of the string, and work toward the irregular areas from the straight line.

6. When you come to a curve, cut the sod to fit the area.

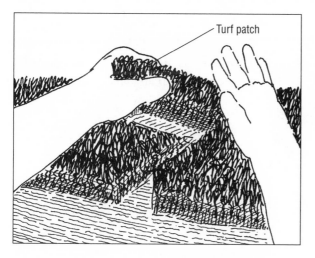

Turf patch

7. Lay the pieces of sod end to end and edge to edge. Place the turves as close together as possible, but do not overlap them. If gaps appear between turves, cut small pieces of sod from a spare turf and insert them where needed.

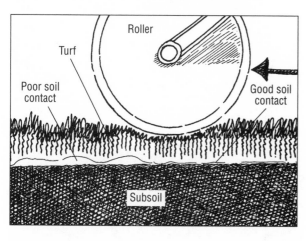

Roller

Turf

Poor soil contact

Good soil contact

Subsoil

8. Roll newly sodded lawn with a light metal roller filled with only a couple of inches of water to ensure good soil contact.

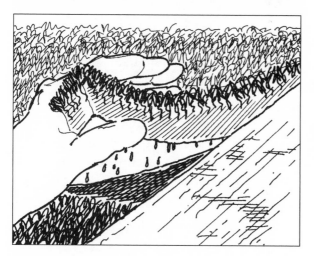

9. Using a sprinkler, water for a half hour every other day for two weeks. If the weather is hot and dry, water every day. Move the sprinkler around for even coverage. The first time you water, lift a corner of the sod to see if soil underneath is soaked. Pay close attention to the edges of sod along walks and driveways; these areas are the first to dry out.

Laying Sod on a Bank

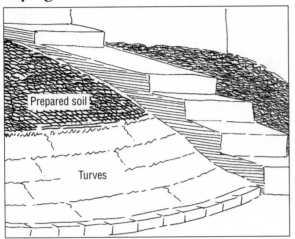

1. Prepare the soil as for the flat lawn area. Lay the first row of sod along the bottom of the bank, and work your way up.

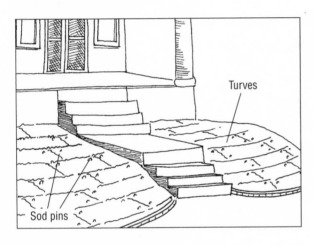

2. Stagger the turves in brickwork style. Place the turves as close together as possible, but do not overlap them.

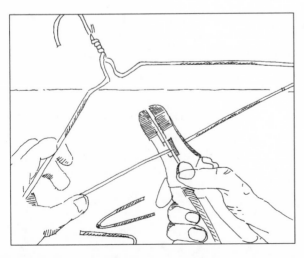

3. Pin turves in place with metal sod pins. You can buy these pins at a garden center or make your own from old coat hangers. Remove them when the turves have knitted. Do so before you mow the area for the first time. Water thoroughly and as necessary until roots are established. After the first watering, lift a corner of the sod to check the moisture of the soil underneath. Do not walk on the bank for two weeks.

Controlling Insects
and Diseases

22

Spraying and Dusting

❧

PLANTS, LIKE ALL LIVING THINGS, are subject to illnesses, and the best treatment is prevention. Keep your beds and borders free of debris that may harbor insects; weed and cultivate your plantings on a regular basis. Spraying and dusting should be considered a last resort. Today's war on pests and diseases offers the gardener a choice: the organic (chemical free) or the inorganic (chemical) approach. Both types of controls are available as liquids in ready-to-use spray containers or dusts in squeeze canisters. These approaches may work for small infestations, but for extensive treatments to be cost-effective, you must mix your own solutions.

The job of controlling plant diseases and infestations is easiest when you have the right equipment and use it correctly. Read labels carefully (before you buy and before you use), follow directions precisely, and store both chemical and nonchemical pesticides and fungicides safely. These weapons have one purpose: to kill.

Organic Pesticides

Household detergents, especially those with a lemon scent, are useful for controlling white flies, aphids, and red spider mites. Use 1 tablespoon per gallon of water.

Rotenone is an old remedy for Mexican bean beetles, aphids, thrips, and chewing insects. Always apply it when the weather is calm, using a duster. Rotenone is toxic to fish and birds.

Ryania controls corn borers and other worms. Follow the manufacturer's directions for application.

Sabadilla controls squash bugs and stink bugs. Use with care; it can irritate the eyes and lungs.

Talcum powder is used to fight flea beetles and corn earworms. A light dusting on leaves after a rainfall should suffice.

Nicotine sulfate (Black Leaf 40) kills soft-bodied sucking insects. It is extremely poisonous and must be used with caution.

Snuff sprinkled on the surface of the soil around houseplants will control flies and worms because of its nicotine content.

Salt sprinkled on slugs and snails will kill them.

Oil and sulfur sprays are applied only on hard or woody plants to control scale, leafhoppers, aphids, and mites. Some are applied only in the dormant season and others during the summer; follow the manufacturer's instructions.

Neem oil is a botanical insecticide derived from the seeds of an Indian tree. It repels Japanese beetles, although it will not kill them. It is harmless to humans.

TOOLS AND SUPPLIES

Plastic spray bottle (trigger or pump type)

Hose-end sprayer

Tank-type compression sprayer

Duster

Plastic milk cartons

Fertilizer spreader

Face mask (kind used for painting)

Disposable surgical gloves

The Best Treatment Is Prevention

• Keep your garden free of debris, such as fallen fruits, branches, twigs, and leaves. Clean borders and beds weekly during the growing season.

• Weed regularly to eliminate places where pests might breed.

• Keep plants well spaced to allow air circulation and to prevent moisture accumulation.

• Whenever possible, buy disease-resistant strains.

• Avoid overhead watering, which would wet the foliage. Don't work in a wet garden.

• Check soil structure and pH annually.

• Don't reuse potting soil.

• Rotate your crops. If an ornamental plant fails to thrive where you plant it, try a new location.

• Encourage birds to live on your property by feeding them in the winter and providing birdhouses in the spring. Birds are great bug catchers. They eat all day long, and feed their young as well. A baby bird consumes three times its own weight in food each day.

Using a Hand-held Sprayer

A hand-held sprayer is best used close up for problems in small areas. It is ideal for house-plants or potted plants growing on a window-sill or in a small greenhouse.

1. Fill sprayer with water, and adjust the spray so that you can adequately cover the foliage of the plant. Add insecticide or fungicide according to the label directions. To avoid disposal problems, don't mix more than you can use.

2. Spray the plants, wetting both sides of the leaves.

Using a Tank-type Compression Sprayer

A tank-type compression sprayer is useful for treating conifers, fruit trees, and ornamental shrubs. This type of sprayer uses a pump to compress the air inside and force water out in a stream. It usually comes in 1- to 3-gallon sizes. Some of these can be worn on your back, but as 1 gallon of water weighs 8 pounds, it can be heavy to carry around the garden. Always wear gloves and a face mask and spray on a windless day.

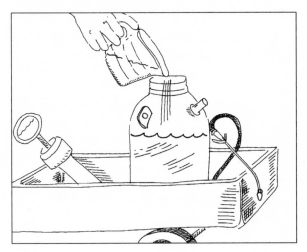

1. Add water to the tank to the desired level, then add the proper ratio of chemical or organic pesticide or fungicide. Don't add the chemical first, or the mixture will foam, making it difficult to monitor the water level. To avoid disposal problems, don't mix more than you can use. Secure the top tightly.

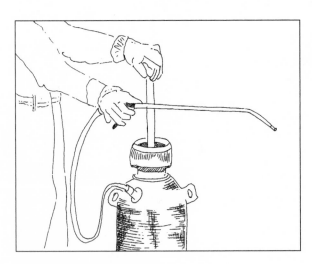

2. Pump air into the container to build up pressure. When it becomes difficult to pump, the pressure is sufficient.

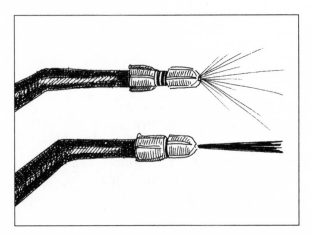

3. Adjust the nozzle to a fine mist for small plants or a stream if you are spraying upward into trees. Don't loosen the nozzle too much, or it might fall off.

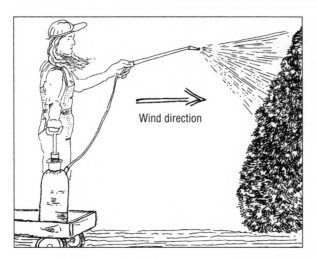

Wind direction

4. Staying upwind of the spray, aim the wand and press the trigger to release the spray mixture. You might have to pump air into the tank to restore pressure several times during an application.

Tips for Spraying

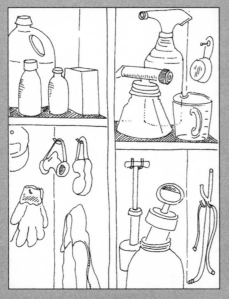

• Always wear a face mask and gloves when operating a sprayer.

• If you use herbicides, to kill poison ivy for example, buy two tanks. Never use the same tank for spraying herbicides and insecticides or fungicides or you may kill desirable plants.

• Thoroughly wash and rinse out all sprayers, wands, and nozzles. Soak the nozzles in hot water to dissolve any deposits that may have accumulated. Store the tank upside down so that it will drain completely and will not accumulate any dust. Never store your tank with a chemical mixture in it.

• If you don't use all of a mixture, store it in a plastic milk carton labeled with the contents and date. If you don't want to save the mixture, take it to a hazardous-waste collection center. The best way to avoid disposal problems is not to buy or mix more of a solution than you can use at one time or in one gardening season.

Using a Hose-end Sprayer

The hose-end sprayer consists of a glass or plastic jar that screws into the end of your garden hose. Some hose-end sprayers have a fixed mixing ratio built into the nozzle; others have a dial on the top that you adjust. The nozzle dilutes the mixture with water as you spray. This type of sprayer is ideal for use on trees and shrubs and usually allows you to adjust your spraying to a fine mist, gentle watering, or long stream.

1. Measure the exact amount of diluted chemical into the jar. Add water according to directions. To avoid disposal problems, do not mix more than you can use.

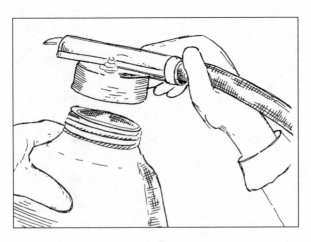

2. Attach the spraying apparatus to your hose, and attach the jar to that, making sure the connections are tight.

3. Turn the hose on and apply the spray to the leaves. Always operate upwind. When finished, thoroughly wash and rinse the container and spraying nozzle.

The Cornell Fungicide Formula

This spray will help prevent or control black spot and mildew on roses, as well as powdery mildew on summer squash, early blight on tomatoes, and alternaria leaf blight on melons.

To one gallon of water, add 1 tablespoon each of baking soda and oil (horticultural oil or vegetable oil) and add the recommended amount of an insecticidal soap for mixing with 1 gallon of water.

Shake well before using and during application. Spray every five to seven days at the first sign of the disease, covering both sides of the leaves with the spray.

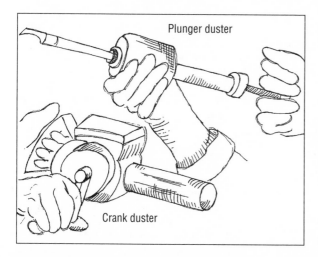

Plunger duster

Crank duster

Using a Duster

To use a *plunger duster,* hold the container in one hand and draw the pump back and forth to dispense the dust. To use a *rotary duster,* or *crank duster,* hold the container in one hand and turn the crank with the other to produce a steady stream of dust. Always wear gloves and a face mask.

Clean dusters by tapping out any accumulation. Lubricate a crank with graphite; oil attracts dust.

Using Fertilizer Spreaders

Fertilizer spreaders may also be used for pesticides. A *drop spreader* is convenient for spreading pesticides over a lawn area and provides the greatest control because you calibrate the hopper to drop the appropriate amount. A *wheeled broadcast spreader* has a rotary wheel that forces the hopper contents out in a wide arc—usually 10 feet. Overlap properly for even distribution of a pesticide. A *hand-held broadcast spreader* is useful for small lawns or rough areas. Turn the crank to spread the contents.

Clean the spreaders thoroughly after use by hosing out the hopper, and place it in the sun to dry.

Seasonal Chores

23

Watering the Garden

❦

PROPER WATERING is one of the most important gardening techniques. There are many variables to be considered: plants' differing moisture needs, the water-retention characteristics of various soils, the effects of wind, temperature, and humidity on soil moisture.

Fresh water can be a scarce commodity in some areas of the country, and you may have to contend with water restrictions. Whatever your circumstances, try not to provide too much or too little water. Too much watering is just as bad as not enough. Overwatering plants makes them susceptible to root rot and smothers plant roots by preventing oxygen from reaching them. Proper watering is a matter of experience. If you spend time in your garden, you will soon perfect your watering skills.

TOOLS AND SUPPLIES

Garden hose	Water wand
Sprinklers	Root feeder
Nozzle	Watering can
Soaker hose	

When to Water

Evening and early morning are the best times to water your garden or lawn because less moisture will be lost through evaporation. Also, winds usually are not as strong in the early-morning or evening, and watering when the air is still will help assure that garden beds on the windward side get their fair share. Between six and eight o'clock in the evening and six and eight in the morning usually are good times. If your plants are susceptible to mildew, however, morning watering is preferable so that the leaves will dry out during the day.

How Much to Water

Soil types vary in their ability to absorb moisture. A friable soil filled with organic matter will absorb nearly all the water that falls on it. Clay soils absorb about three times as much as sandy soils, but drainage is slow. If your garden has clay soil, let your beds dry out partially before watering again because of the slow drainage. If you have amended the soil in your flower beds and vegetable garden well before planting, and applied mulch, half the watering battle is won.

Most vegetables and flowering plants need 1 inch of water per week if mature, and perhaps more if they have just been transplanted in a new environment.

Watering the Lawn

If your footprints remain after you walk across the lawn, it's time to water. Attach a sprinkler to your garden hose and move it about the lawn; try to minimize overlap without neglecting any spots. A lawn should be watered to a 6-inch depth; with average soils, that corresponds to about 1 inch of applied water. Placing a tuna can or flat-bottomed dish near the sprinkler will help you gauge how much water your lawn is getting.

Watering Trees and Shrubs

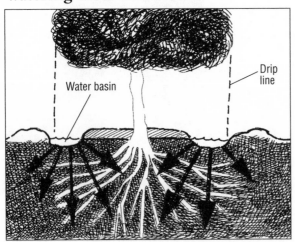

Even established trees and shrubs during dry spells may need to be watered. This supplementary water must reach the root zone of your plants. Use a trowel or hoe to construct a basin about 6 inches wide and 3 inches deep around each tree or shrub. Allow the water from a hose to trickle slowly around the basin during dry spells. If you have mulched your trees and shrubs, put mulch in the basin also. This basin will direct water to the root zone. Soak this area for several hours during dry weather.

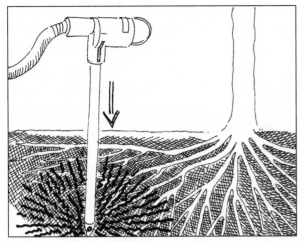

For deep watering, use a root feeder. This tool attaches to a garden hose and acts like a giant hypodermic needle, directing water down a narrow cylinder to the root zone. Insert the tube of the feeder as deep as possible directly around the mulched area of a tree or shrub. Water pressure from the hose will supply moisture 2 to 3 feet underground where it is needed. Move the feeder around the plant at timed intervals, until all the deep roots have been saturated thoroughly. This is an excellent tool to use during severe droughts, because no water is wasted. Always apply extra water to newly planted evergreen trees and shrubs during a dry fall, or prolonged periods of alternate freezing and thawing during the winter, especially if snow cover is light, can lead to severe damage.

Watering Ground-level Gardens

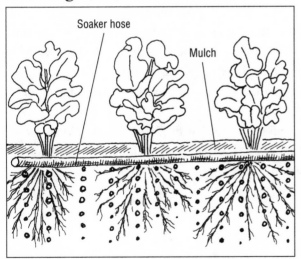

Soaker hose

Mulch

When watering ground-level gardens, make certain water reaches the root zone. Avoid frequent shallow watering. A mere sprinkling with the hose simply brings roots to the surface of the soil in search of moisture. Deep roots, well watered, can better withstand temperature fluctuations and have a better chance for survival. Each time you irrigate, aim for the entire root area and the top foot of soil. The frequency with which you need to water will depend on mulches and the weather.

Place a soaker hose under your mulch and turn it on. Water will slowly trickle down to the root zone, and plant foliage will not be exposed to spraying water. Wet foliage can invite disease (especially during hot, humid weather) or leaf burn, and can weigh down flowering stalks.

Watering Raised Beds

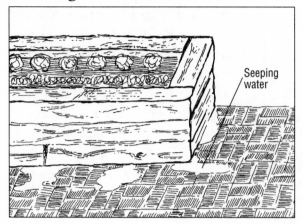

Seeping water

Plants growing in raised beds dry out more quickly during hot summers than plants in ground-level beds. Mulch raised beds heavily, and provide enough water that it seeps out the bottom of the structure.

Watering Container Plants

How often you water a container plant depends on the soil mixture, the type of container, its location, and your climate. Feel the surface of the soil to see if it is dry. Containers on a patio or balcony exposed to full sun may need watering twice a day. When you water, use a watering can or a water wand with a soft-flow nozzle. Never use a strong jet of water on container plants, or you may gouge holes in the soil and expose the roots.

When a root ball gets too dry, the soil sometimes shrinks away from the sides of the pot and the water runs out the drainage holes without reaching the roots. If this occurs, repot the plant in a larger pot to provide more growing space or loosen the soil around the top, then soak with water. If the container is small, submerge it in a bucket of water until bubbles stop rising.

If the pot is in a saucer, empty the saucer after the pot has finished draining. Roots of potted plants need oxygen and will die if they stand in water. If the container is too large to lift, use a turkey baster to remove water from the saucer.

24

Preparing the Garden and Lawn
for Winter

୫ఎ

WINTER NEVER COMES WITHOUT WARNING. Several nights of light frost nip the leaves, and
the lawn glistens in the early-morning sunlight with stretches of white frost. Every plant in
your garden has a minimum temperature it can endure without serious damage or death. If
you garden where winters are severe, you must protect young trees, shrubs, foundation
plantings, roses, and perennials from snow and cold weather. Covering your plants will help
protect them from frost. In a hard-freeze region, mulch heavily to prevent frost from pene-
trating deep into the ground. Perennials need to be mulched to prevent heaving from alternate freezing and thawing.

There are other things you should do before the first snow to prepare your garden and
lawn for winter: rake leaves, weed flower borders, fertilize the lawn. Now is the time to
divide perennials, such as peonies and daylilies. Hill your roses and wrap the trunks of young
trees if you have problems with rodents. Fall is also an excellent time for planting evergreens
and trimming hedges one last time. In zones 4 through 6, you have September, October, and
early November for carrying out these chores. Zone 4 gardeners should get an early start on
wintering; zone 5 gardeners can procrastinate a little.

This chapter is set up as a monthly timetable for fall. Many of the procedures involved in
winterizing your garden are explained in other chapters. Refer to the appropriate chapters
as you prepare to put your garden to bed.

September Chores
The Lawn
- Rake leaves and compost them (see Chapter 4).
- Apply a nitrogen-rich fertilizer, such as 20–10–10, 16–8–8, 14–7–7, 10–6–4, or 10–5–5, using a drop spreader. Apply no more than 2 pounds per 1,000 square feet at one time. Spread it evenly when the lawn is dry; do not overlap. Water the lawn immediately after application to prevent burning the grass blades.

The Flower Garden
- Continue watering the garden as needed.
- Pull weeds and replenish mulch where necessary.
- Pull out spent annuals. If they are free of disease, compost them (see Composting).
- Pick the spent blooms on perennials. The plants should be staked securely (see Staking and Tying).
- Divide and plant peonies, daylilies, and creeping phlox (see Dividing Perennials).
- Plant spring-flowering bulbs (see Planting Bulbs).
- Dig up tender bulbs, such as tuberous begonias and caladiums (and dahlias in zone 6 and lower), after the first frost. Store them in a cool, dry place in sand, peat, or vermiculite to prevent shriveling.

The Vegetable Garden
- Water late-fall crops as needed.
- Pull weeds and replenish mulch where necessary.
- Pull out spent plants, as they may harbor disease.
- Continue insect control. Insect populations tend to increase in late summer (see Spraying and Dusting).
- Spread manure or compost over unused garden space.

Woody Plants
- Clip hedges for the last time (see Pruning).
- Continue insect control. Use dormant oil spray on pines with scale or red spider infestations (see Spraying and Dusting).
- Plant evergreens (see Planting Trees).

October Chores
The Lawn
- Continue mowing and raking leaves as necessary.

The Flower Garden
- After a killing frost, remove dead plants. Compost them if they are free of disease (see Composting).

• Dig up all summer bulbs. Store them in a cool, dry place in sand, peat, or vermiculite to prevent shriveling.

  • Plant tulips and other spring bulbs (see Planting Bulbs).

  • Begin forcing bulbs (see Planting Bulbs).

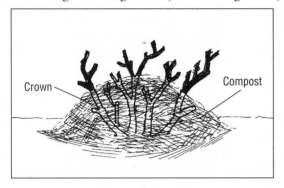

Crown — Compost

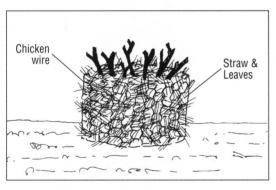

Chicken wire — Straw & Leaves

• If you plant new, bare-root roses during October, hill them for winter by placing several shovelfuls of compost or topsoil over their crowns or encircle each plant with a cylinder of chicken wire 1 foot high and 1 foot in diameter, and fill it with a mixture of straw and leaves. If your winters are mild and temperatures do not drop below 10 to 20 degrees F., simply rake extra mulch around the crowns. If your established roses are still blooming, you may wait until November to cut, tie, and mulch them.

Woody Plants

  • Plant deciduous trees and shrubs (see Planting Trees).

  • If the fall has been dry, water evergreen trees and shrubs.

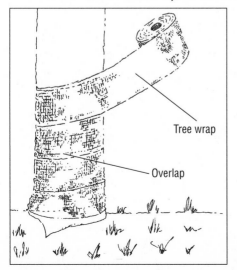

Tree wrap

Overlap

• Wrap trunks of young trees to prevent sunscald or rodent damage. To do this, you will need sharp scissors, strips of burlap or commercial tree wrap, a 1-by-2-foot piece of perforated plastic, and twine.

1. Cut strips of burlap 2 inches wide or use commercial tree wrap from a garden center. Beginning at the bottom of the trunk, wrap the burlap around the trunk up to the first branch, overlapping 1 inch at each turn.

2. To secure the wrap, tie a piece of twine around the top or push a galvanized nail through the burlap. Take care not to scrape the trunk.

Galvanized nail

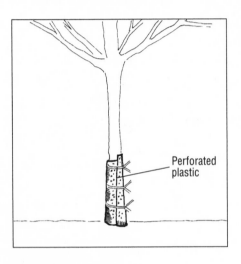

3. If you have rodent problems, wrap the trunk 1 foot above the snow line with a piece of perforated plastic.

Perforated plastic

November Chores

The Lawn

• Continue to rake up leaves and compost.

The Flower Garden

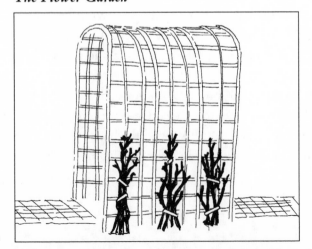

• Cut back tea, shrub, floribunda, and grandiflora roses that have been flowering all season to 24 inches, and tie canes of climbers to avoid wind damage. Clean up fallen leaves from roses; these may harbor black spot spores.

• Place an open, porous mulch such as straw or pine boughs over perennials after the ground is frozen. If you can wait until January, cut Christmas trees make a great cover for perennial beds.

• Cover bulb beds with compost or well-rotted manure.

The Vegetable Garden

• Remove stakes. If you used newspaper or brown paper mulches in the garden, incorporate them into the soil so that they won't find their way into your neighbors' yards.

• Spread compost or manure over the garden. Till it in by hand or use a cultivator.

Woody Plants

• Water evergreen trees and shrubs again if the weather has been dry.

• Prune trees and shrubs as necessary (see Pruning).

• Mulch young rooted shrub cuttings after the first hard freeze (see Taking Cuttings).

• Where winters are severe, cover evergreen shrubs with burlap to prevent sunscald and snow damage. You will need burlap, heavy twine or string, and scissors.

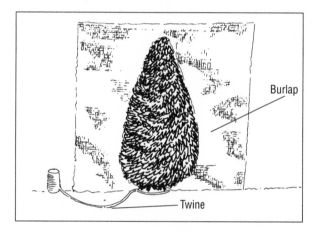

Burlap

Twine

1. With a helper, cut a strip of burlap to fit snugly around the entire shrub from bottom to top. Tie the loose end of a ball of twine to the bottom of the shrub at ground level.

2. With a helper, drape the burlap around the shrub, and begin to pull the twine up and around the burlap covering. Walk around the shrub with the ball of twine in your hands, winding the string higher with each loop, allowing 6 to 8 inches between loops.

3. When you reach the top, tie the twine securely around the burlap.

Miscellaneous Chores

• Clean, sharpen, and store shovels, hoes, trowels, and spades. Use a wire brush or steel wool on metal parts, then oil and grease them.

• Clean the lawn mower, empty the gas tank, and store for the winter.

• Clean out birdhouses and make any necessary repairs.

• Set up bird-feeding stations.

Selecting Tools

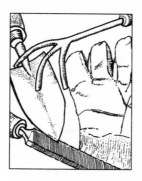

25

Basic Tools

᠁

BEFORE YOU BUY ANY TOOL—manual or powered—determine whether your use of the tool will justify its cost and the space you must allow for its storage. Do you really need it? Okay: Find the right size and weight for you. If it doesn't feel right, don't buy it. You can accomplish much more, for example, with a smaller garden fork that doesn't tire you out than with a large one that is awkward to use. Always invest in good quality; ignore bargain tools. If you are on a budget, buy one tool at a time, but always buy the best.

Tools with Long Handles

Spades and Shovels

Stainless steel spades and shovels are the best, though they're the most expensive. Soil, no matter how sticky, will fall off the polished surface, making your job easier. If you can't afford stainless steel, buy forged-steel spades and shovels, and keep them clean. A die stamp on the tool will indicate that the steel has been forged. Never buy pressed steel, which will bend and distort under pressure.

Buy a size that suits you. A long handle allows you to stand more erect and lessens back strain. A shorter handle that ends in a **D** shape is good for working in a crowded bed. The angle between the wood handle and the blade is also important. The more pronounced the angle, the greater the leverage when scooping heavy soil. A round-nosed shovel is better for scooping, a square-end spade for digging and edging.

Garden Fork

The digging fork is another valuable tool for all-purpose use in the garden. Buy one that is made of forged steel and fitted with a wooden handle. The tines and base of a garden fork are usually made as a single, cast-iron unit. Never buy pressed steel, which will bend under pressure. The more expensive English-made garden fork is square-tined and heavier than a flat-tined fork. Buy what suits you.

Garden Rake and Lawn Rake

Garden rakes have short tines and are square backed or bowed. Either type is useful for breaking up clods of soil, spreading compost and mulch, and preparing a seed bed. Buy a garden rake made from forged steel for durability and longevity. Don't buy one with more than twelve tines, or it can be heavy and awkward to use.

Lawn rakes, leaf rakes, have long, flexible tines. They are useful for raking leaves, removing dead thatch, raking in grass seed after sowing, and general garden cleanup.

Garden Hoes

Buy two garden hoes: a Dutch hoe, for pushing backward and forward when weeding, and a 6-inch-wide, conventional garden hoe, for all-purpose cultivating. The handles must be long enough for you to work upright to avoid back strain.

Watering and Spraying Tools

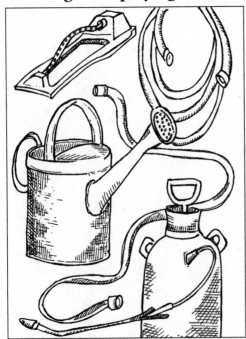

Watering Can

Buy the largest and best watering can you can find and afford, keeping in mind that it will be heavier when filled with water. Stainless steel will last indefinitely. A fine nozzle attachment, called a rose, is useful for watering seedlings.

Hoses

Buy the best hose—one that will not kink. The larger the diameter, the more water you can deliver. A 5/8-inch hose is the most popular size for lawns and gardens. Store your hose on a reel, preferably a through-feed type, which allows you to unroll just what you need.

A soaker hose is useful but optional. This type of hose is designed to drip water slowly along its length. You can leave it permanently in position under mulch, and turn it on when you think necessary.

Sprinkler

Select a sprinkler that suits your needs. One that has a fine spray pattern and will provide both short and long sweeps is most practical.

Sprayer

A pressure sprayer is optional but useful as your gardening efforts expand. A pressure sprayer with a pump handle usually holds up to 3 gallons of solution, and you can use it with a shoulder strap. The nozzle adjusts to a spray mist or a high-pressure stream, and the sprayer has a wand for reaching high areas.

Cutting Tools

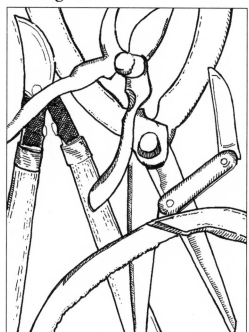

Pruners

Scissor-type hand-held pruning shears are used for cutting stems up to $1/2$ inch in diameter. Scissor types, in which the blades overlap, are preferable because they provide closer, cleaner cuts. Look for sturdily made pruners with high-quality carbon-steel blades. They should feel good in your hand, especially if they operate with a spring mechanism that reopens the pruners after each cut.

Lopping Shears

Lopping shears, or loppers, are long-handled pruners that provide extra leverage for cutting branches $1/2$ to $11/2$ inches in diameter. These shears are especially good for cutting out suckers at the base of shrubs and for thinning young branches on trees. They should have carbon-steel, nonstick coated blades and a shock-absorbing bumper. If there is no bumper, your arms will have to take the shock.

Hedge Shears

Hedge shears are used for trimming hedges with branches up to $1/2$ inch in diameter; don't use them for other pruning chores. Pay the price for carbon-steel blades, which will hold a good, sharp edge. The hedge shears should have a shock-absorbing bumper to lessen jarring and forearm fatigue.

Pruning Saw

Any branches larger than 1 1/2 inches in diameter should be cut with a pruning saw. These small, curved, narrow-blade saws sometimes have teeth on both sides. All are excellent and rarely need to be sharpened.

Pocketknife

A pocketknife is one of the most useful tools in the garden. Buy one that fits comfortably into your pocket, and keep it sharp. Use a carborundum stone for sharpening your pocketknife.

Hand Tools

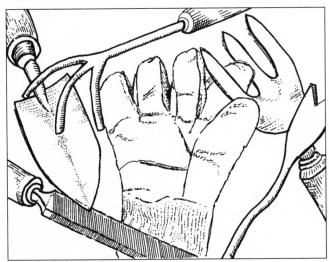

Hand Cultivator

A hand cultivator with three curved tines made from chrome-plated forged steel and a wood handle is the best. This is an excellent tool for loosening soil in tightly planted areas to provide aeration.

Hand Fork

The hand fork is a multipurpose tool useful for loosening compacted soil or digging up small plants by the roots. The hand fork can be used for digging out an entire clump of weeds, roots and all.

Trowel

The trowel is one of the most personal of garden tools. Shop around until you find one that is comfortable in your hands; it should be light enough to handle with ease. The drop-shank variety, with an angle between the handle and blade, is preferred by most gardeners. Buy a good one made from heat-treated steel that will not bend when you thrust it into the ground. It should last a lifetime.

Gloves

Sturdy leather gloves are essential for all-purpose work in the garden. Soft, expensive goatskin gloves feel comfortable but will not protect your hands from thorns and heavy gardening chores. Use vinyl or rubber gloves for handling chemicals.

File

Buy a good file, and use it regularly to sharpen your tools. Sharp tools will make your work in the garden much easier. A metal file or rasp is appropriate for sharpening a shovel; use a whetstone for tools with finer edges.

Index